Dispute Management

Dispute Management

◆

How to End the Litigation Problem

David U. Strawn

iUniverse, Inc.
New York Lincoln Shanghai

Dispute Management
How to End the Litigation Problem

iUniverse, Inc.

For information address:
iUniverse, Inc.
2021 Pine Lake Road, Suite 100
Lincoln, NE 68512
www.iuniverse.com

ISBN: 0-595-30493-1 (pbk)
ISBN: 0-595-66174-2 (cloth)

Printed in the United States of America

Contents

Appendices

Introduction

Other writers have chronicled the ills of the American court system more than adequately. This book will not add to that literature. It is instead about what we can do to change the system to function in the work and personal worlds in which you and I live.

We have crowded ourselves because we like being in close proximity to other humans. We are herd animals. We like living and working together. Our ability to do so has been one of the sources of our evolutionary success and our reproductive victory amid life on earth.

If you run with the herd, as we do, you expect to be bumped—and to bump back. Sometimes the bumps we give and receive are too hard to ignore. Conflict develops, and some conflicts cannot be handled one-on-one. Because we are the brightest of all the cooperating animals on earth, we have invented ways to resolve conflict.

In our times, we have chosen to use courts that are provided by the government for resolution of the conflicts we choose not to personally resolve, and we find ourselves dissatisfied with our choice. What's wrong?

The fundamental cause of trouble with the court system is you and me. We have, particularly in the mid and late twentieth century, delegated too many of our disputes to lawyers and the courts for handling. We—and the lawyers, administrators, scholars and judges responsible for managing the courts—have failed to recognize that the ancient system could not handle the work we were giving it.

The people responsible for the system looked to their unique, discrete bodies of knowledge for answers. Among many suggested solutions, we find the following themes.

Lawyers sought the answer in more rules and statutes. From 1955 to 1995, the Florida Rules of Procedure (regulating the management of law suits and appeals) grew from a scant booklet to a major volume: from fewer than one hundred pages to almost one thousand pages of rules and forms.

Judges thought "more judges" were the answer. Court systems nationwide beseeched legislative bodies to appropriate funds for additional judges. The judges argued that the case-backlog was caused by too few judges. They did not consider that the system itself was the cause of the backlog.

Scholars thought keeping cases out of court might hold the answer. "Diversions" were suggested for sending cases away from the courthouse to community resources. Some thought judges could more closely manage their caseloads, leading to more settlements and fewer trials.

Administrators hoped that efforts to track cases and shorten case life by watching judges closely would relieve the system.

Each profession saw symptoms, and attacked the symptoms they saw. None understood the underlying problem, although a few of the scholars came close to finding the solution.

I wrote this book in plain language. I know how to write things in scholarly language, but this is a call to act—now. It is not a call for "discussions." Many of you are people able to initiate immediate action to begin correction of the problem. You are in positions of leadership. You will be able to bring about quick changes in the organizations you lead.

You, whoever you may be, can begin by immediately changing your life and the lives of your families, colleagues and friends.

This book will provide you with fundamental ideas about how communities and individuals can better approach dispute resolution. It will provide positive and effective guidance to minimize the incidence and duration of lawsuits in America. Other writers will, and should, expand the discussion of these concepts.

The concepts and methods explained in this book have been proven to work. A few thousand people, trained by my company and me are applying them personally and professionally. Several states have begun the work of applying these concepts. In Florida, we have applied several of the basic concepts, beginning with legislation adopted in 1987. By 1994, these methods had resulted in an estimated eighty per cent reduction in the number of cases which judges and juries were required to decide. By 2003, we found mediation the primary forum for dispute resolution in Florida.

A few corporations are using the methods, and are being rewarded by huge financial savings and reduced friction with those with whom they deal, as well as with their employees.

As a beginning, we should start with ourselves. I hope that you will apply these ideas, as you can, to your reality. That would be a wonderful first step toward a better world.

Let's get moving. We can help our ailing, but not terminally ill legal system!

1

The Problem—We don't take responsibility for our disputes

As a nation, as business and professional people and in our personal lives, we have been passive about how our disputes are processed and who processes them.

Passive, but extraordinarily interested. Active in our complaints and criticisms, but passive when it comes to doing something about the problem.

The price of looking the other way, of letting others handle our disputes, has been high. We have forfeited important personal and cultural values.

It isn't that we have been irresponsible. It's just that we have entrusted too much of our lives to government. We delegated management of our disputes to others: lawyers, judges and the courts. They accepted the work gratefully and in good faith. We did it in good faith and in a sense of preserving institutions. We conserved. After all, that's the way we had "always" done it.

Even after the Rodney King and O.J. Simpson trials, we simply complained and carped over what messes they were. We groused that it only took the Simpson *criminal case* jury four hours to decide the "issues" of a nine-month-long debacle. We then see Simpson found responsible for murder and liable for enormous damages for his wrongs by a second jury in a *civil* trial.

We watch with suspicion as lawyers and judges plaster the eight-hundred-year old beast of the adversary trial with juristic poultices. We are fearful, as radical and reactionary alike attempt to kill the creature because of its failures in handling cases like the King and Simpson cases to our satisfaction.

If offered no alternative to the adversary trial method, we will preserve the adversary trial, lonely in its courthouse cage. We will groan under the burden of social needs unresolved and march along as we have, none the better, perhaps the worse.

Or will we? Is there hope for a better way? Could we find a beginning here? A new way which is more than another punctuation of an interminable and unsatisfactory history of dispute resolution: the "English" way? We Americans have invented so much that is new and good. Why not take a look at how we should manage our disputes?

The point of beginning lies in understanding that we should not simply seek alternatives to the adversary method. It is not a question of this method *or* that. Rather, we should look first as to why we have courts at all. Then we should examine what disputes there are, which ones we want the courts to handle, and by what methods we want disputes handled. Could it be that one method will better handle some disputes than another, some better handled privately, than by government? Some better handled by lawyers and judges, and others preferably handled by other professionals?

We could, and we can take charge. This book is about why we haven't and how we could. It insists that we should either take charge or stop complaining about trials, judges, lawyers, and waiting for "fairness" and "justice" to somehow happen on their own.

As you'll see when you read Chapter 4, "How We Got This Way," we have drifted on a current deflected from native channels by the Norman invasion of England many centuries ago. Although our present governmental system of dispute resolution is one founded by England's Norman rulers, others have perpetuated and protected the power-concentrating devices of the system.

We, the otherwise amazingly independent American people, have permitted one occupational group to dictate the means of dispute resolution to our entire community.

I speak as a lawyer. I am a member of the occupation that rules over virtually all of the dispute resolution devices available to the American public. As doctors own your health life, we lawyers own the life of your disputes. While you live, we doctors and lawyers profit from you troubles. In death the doctors lose out, but lawyers get one last shot at your "estate." The system is designed and managed so that you must turn to us in your efforts to avoid disputes from contracts and legislation and for help when other disputes erupt.

As a lawyer, former judge and law teacher, I think it's time you took charge. I don't think people with my peculiar education are the only ones suited to manage disputes. I think you should manage your disputes, using people like me only as a resource.

For more than three decades, I have struggled with what might be done to craft a better system of resolving conflict. In the sixties I became aware that the United States' court systems are based upon a fundamental fallacy. The American system only offered *adversary trials* as a means of resolving disputes—*all* disputes. I knew by then that the one-bottle-cures-all approach offered by our courts was insufficient. Divorces weren't the same as contract suits that weren't at all like larceny cases, nor were they like suits for personal injury damages. What system would be better? How could the system be repaired?

Educated and socialized as a lawyer, I first looked for answers within the legal system. That is where we lawyers are trained to look. Then, I couldn't visualize that the subtle trail to answers for such questions could exist outside legal literature. In my professional arrogance, I assumed that all there was to know could be found in a law library.

Legal lore let me down. Legal scholars seemed only interested in revisions to the adversary system. Critical examination of the system and its role in culture, in community, and what might be *systemically* altered was unnecessary for most, heresy for others.

In the early seventies I began to look beyond the borders of the legal system.

My first insight came from learning in 1971 that in England a special Commission of the Archbishop of Canterbury had reported that mediation could be better used than courts to address the needs of couples when their marriages dissolved. What little literature I could find (none of it in the collections of law libraries at the time) seemed always to see all methods of dispute resolution other than adversary trials as *alternative dispute resolution.*

Why couldn't mediation become the *primary* method of dispute resolution?

In 1972 I wrote a monograph, urging people, when they wanted a divorce, something like mediation should be incorporated into what courts could offer to the public. I could not find a publisher. I should have known. In 1972, the word mediation could not be found as a separate index item in any of the major legal indexes. The only reference I found to the word was as a subset of information about labor law. Mediation was then of little interest to lawyers and legal scholars.

Sixteen years later I saw my home state, Florida, adopt a law permitting our courts to *order* litigants to mediate their disputes with trained and "certified" court mediators. What brought about the change?

Although my monograph remains unpublished to this day, it had its effect. It had continued to interest non-lawyers, then a handful of progressive, thinking lawyers in Florida's legislature. It was extensively quoted in calls for reform of the way we treated dissolving marriages.

In the mid-eighties, the Florida Legislature created a "Legislative Study Commission on Alternative Dispute Resolution for the Courts." I was Chair of the Commission for its two-year life. I drafted and signed the documents setting out its legislative plan for modification of our court system.

The plan called for a fundamental, systemic revision of Florida's court system. It called for a system providing both mediation and arbitration, in addition to the adversary trial. In 1987, Florida's legislature adopted laws implementing the essential elements of the plan, leaving final design and implementation to the courts.

In 1988 I was called by the Supreme Court of Florida to act as first Chair of the newly created Mediation and Arbitration Rules Committee. In that work, I saw Florida become the first American State to adopt the concept that courts could offer more than adversary trials alone, and be better for it. By 1989, Florida's courts had become the first of America's courts to depart from the Anglo-Saxon heritage of permitting citizens only adversary trials as means for resolving their disputes.

Texas quickly, then Indiana, North Carolina and South Carolina followed the same path. Tennessee is implementing a program as well. Other states have been hesitantly experimenting with adoption of similar laws, crafting similar changes to their court system. More will come.

How effective is the modification? Of the population of all cases filed in Florida, only an estimated one to two per cent now require disposition by a judge or jury. Historically, about five to six per cent of the lawsuits filed ultimately require a trial or final hearing before a judge.

Does it cost the state more to use the system? No. The system has reduced the cost of the justice system for civil cases in Florida by flattening the demand for judges and courtrooms, despite the continued growth of Florida's population. The system ends cases faster than the old system. Faster is cheaper in litigation. The new system saves the public money, but saves money for litigants as well. Insurance companies are ardent in their support of the system, even propagating it in other states. Cases cost them less to handle in this environment than in the traditional one, where adversary trials are the only forum for resolution of cases when face-to-face negotiation fails.

Does the modification of the system result in higher costs to litigants? No. Litigants pay the mediators and arbitrators, not the state. Cases end sooner, without the need for preparing and presenting trials.

Legal economists have long known that the longer a file remains open, the more the case will cost. Mediators in Florida have helped end many cases before lawsuits were even filed. Insurance companies report millions of dollars in savings on legal fees and costs since the inception of the new Florida court system.

The Florida system is presently limited to civil cases. It is not applied to criminal cases. In Chapter 9 we will explore how the system could be extended to criminal cases as well. These thoughts will be among the most controversial in this book. Rightly so, as concepts such as the presumption of innocence of the accused and the burden on the State that it prove its charges beyond reasonable doubt are constitutional essentials.

Dispute Management calls for cultural change as well as individual change. It requires that we debate not only *who* should resolve disputes, but *by what process* they should be resolved. If we are to improve criminal justice, as we have seen civil justice enhanced in Florida, we must be willing to debate and change constitutional principles of longstanding.

Recent history demonstrates the success of modifications to a governmental system for dispute resolution. We can and must go beyond modifications to court systems; they are only a subset of the resources available to manage our disputes. We must take charge not only of our courts, but of our private organizations and personal lives as well. The only system that will be satisfactory is a comprehensive one. We can no longer leave dispute resolution entirely to our governments.

While writing this book, I often felt angry. On reflection, I dismissed my anger. Whose fault was it that the system works as it does? My ancestors, my predecessors. Mine too. How can I be angry at a dog for barking or a bee for stinging? How can I be angry with neighbors and colleagues who believe the American court system and its attendant legal profession are *all* we need?

I would be angry with myself if I had failed to voice the ideas found in this book. The precepts, methods, and management ideas written here were the source of, and are demonstrated in a system now at work in Florida. These ideas can be spread to help cure the illness of, and our excessive dependence upon a formal governmental system of dispute resolution. These are ideas that can be used to aid organizations and individuals to take charge of inevitable disputes and to manage them.

Dispute Management is the key.

2

What is "Dispute Management" and Why Use It?

What is "Dispute Management" and why do we need it? *Who* needs it? Isn't that what the courts and lawyers handle for us?

Take this for a fact—if you are living with other humans, disputes occur daily. Most will be minor, some will be personal, others related to economics. Just two people may be involved, or a larger group. Life-threatening, career-damaging, emotionally difficult disputes are part of your personal and business or professional life.

How have you managed your disputes in the past? Have you had a *plan*? How have you prepared yourself for the inevitable?

You ignored some of these disputes. Others you treated light-heartedly, and agreed with what the other person wanted. Some found you in serious negotiation with the other person. Still others seemed insoluble when you tried to work them out, one on one. These may have led to the loss of a personal or business relationship.

Some of your disputes you may have referred to lawyers. These referrals led to costly, often frustrating processes. By the time the law finished chewing up your problem, you couldn't recognize it anymore!

In the business world, people do all of the things individuals do, but the dodge to lawyers is more common. In large organizations, the referral can be to in-house counsel; in smaller ones, to an outside attorney.

As you were growing up, and later learning your job and making a career, did you educate yourself about negotiation? You jog or work out to keep your body fit, but how have you trained for negotiation?

What have you done to be "in shape" for handling serious disputes? Are you familiar with appropriate use of multiple types of dispute resolution processes? Do you understand how to organize a series of dispute resolution processes into a *system*?

Probably you acknowledge that as common as disputing is, you have done little to prepare for life's disputes. We dispute constantly. In our search for the perfect marriage, we divorce each other at a rapid pace, but does anyone teach us how to do it more gracefully, less expensively, and more competently? A few public schools have recently realized that negotiation skills are vital to everyday life. Colleges and universities, even graduate schools, take no time for teaching students how to cope with disputes.

However, you say, the law schools are training the people who will handle our worst disputes! We don't have to know, because they will know and will guide us.

Two problems here. First, not all law schools train students to negotiate or to understand various "alternative dispute resolution" (ADR) methods. Those who do offer negotiation and ADR training as a brief course as an "elective." Your lawyer may have no more training or experience in negotiating and sophisticated use of ADR than you do. That strongly suggests that your referral to a lawyer is likely to get you into court, where negotiating skills are not required. Persuasive skills are all that is required in court. Court is what lawyers prefer and what they are most familiar with.

Interestingly, the majority of law school faculties and deans don't think knowing how to negotiate, mediate, or arbitrate and even knowing how to try a law suit are important to students or to the public they intend to serve! Such "clinical" courses have low status and are not given much time. Medical schools insist that a doctor personally view the inside of a human body, but law schools rarely require a student to look at the inside of a courtroom.

The second problem, and the principle reason for this book is the assumption that, "The lawyers will handle disputes for us; therefore we

don't need to know all this stuff." I think we have for too long delegated too many serious and major aspects of our personal, business and
community lives to lawyers and the courts. There are options and alternatives, but we haven't been educated about them and we have not
been trained to use them.

Dispute Management is about these options and alternatives and
how they can be woven into a system that will greatly improve the
function of the courts and the way we handle our disputes.

Dispute Management is taking responsibility for the disputes that
individuals, businesses and governments simply cannot avoid. It is
more than having a line in your budget for "legal expense."

What do I mean, "taking responsibility" for disputes? I mean not
hiding your head in the sand or simply crumbling when someone
wants to stand in your way or when you have an argument over something. I mean taking positive charge of your life and your organization's life, in anticipating disputes, knowing what is likely to come
your way, and having a plan for dealing with the dispute before it happens. I mean requiring government court systems and the lawyers that
run them to change in order to provide the processes we need to give us
a chance to manage our disputes.

Dispute Management is pro-active, not reactive. It acknowledges
that disputes will come your way. It is a method for anticipating these
disputes, understanding their characteristics and the needs of those
who bring them to your door. Dispute Management recognizes that it
is people who make disputes difficult or easy to resolve, not the dispute
itself. Different people will respond to different dispute resolution processes and techniques. Dispute Management requires that the devices
and procedures be in place, with trained people (including you and
me) ready to use them to better manage our disputes.

Dispute Management recognizes that there is an extensive catalog of
dispute resolution mechanisms available, and that some of them are
better suited to certain kinds of disputes. Dispute Management knows
that systems for managing disputes may be more effective than stand-

alone use of a single process. One bottle does not cure all. Dispute Management deals with the order of use of processes, as well as the identification of discrete processes.

"Sue the bastards!" is too simplistic for the dispute manager. The dispute manager has a plan for getting past the people and on to identification and resolution of the problem. This person knows that thoughtful techniques and processes will resolve most conflicts. S/he knows that brandishing rules of law is a last gasp, desperate move for the incompetent bargainer. S/he knows that courts, laws and precedents should be reserved for cases involving incompetent negotiators, pathological fighters (those lawyers and clients that would rather fight than win), and for matters requiring a community, business or personal precedent.

Dispute Management means having a plan: an intelligently contrived plan, with knowledge of available resources and an understanding of the cost of alternatives.

Don't be surprised by disputes. It is not a question of "if I have a serious dispute." It is better to face up and plan for "when I have a serious dispute."

Articulate your plan's goals. They could be:

To avoid disputes

To avoid some kinds of disputes

To keep the cost of handling disputes to a minimum

To keep my customers, even when disputes happen

To keep from losing still other customers because of a customer dispute

To use disputes constructively to build better relationships

To let me make more friends

To maintain high levels of employee and executive morale

To avoid having the government make decisions for me or my company

To stay out of court

Dispute Management for a business will have different objectives than Dispute Management for a unit of government, such as a state or city. Dispute Management for individuals will differ from Dispute Management for both kinds of organizations.

The first few chapters of this book identify the roots of the problem and will help you understand the process courts use. You will then learn what tools are available for working on the problem and will come to understand a basic method for Dispute Management. Then we'll apply the method to see just how a government, a business organization, and an individual might apply these concepts to begin actively managing the population of disputes that each faces. We will also explore two areas of law in which Dispute Management is needed terribly: criminal law and divorce.

Taken together, the chapters will provide a new orientation as to how disputes can be handled, and will provide a framework for the changes we should make. Application of Dispute Management principles gives us cause for real hope for the future of America's courts, the bar, and those who need their services.

3

Taking Inventory—What are the methods of dispute resolution?

To design our system, it will be helpful to learn of as many dispute resolution processes as possible. We recognize that different people and different disputes may respond more readily to different kinds of dispute resolution processes.

We will list a menu of dispute resolution devices that our ancestors and other cultures have used. We'll begin with the simplest, least expensive and most common, and progress to the most complicated, expensive and unusual.

Conciliation

When this method is used, no bargaining or negotiation occurs. One says to another, "Look, you were my best friend when this argument started. I want you to be my best friend when it is done. I hear myself repeating all my old reasons for why we should do it my way. Can we sleep on it, and take it up again tomorrow after work?"

Conciliation is used to maintain and enhance relationships. Ordinary psychological processes often bring about resolution of the dispute when conciliation is achieved.

Every salesperson knows that relationships must be in place, however transitory and shallow they may be, before negotiation can effectively begin.

Negotiation

When we have disputes, we try to work things out by finding mutually acceptable answers. Sometimes one will try to win something from the other through negotiation.

While negotiating, smart bargainers work at maintaining relationships with each other, sometimes to meet each other's needs, sometimes just to gain whatever advantages may come to the bargainer for having kept the relationship in place.

Negotiation is different in different parts of the world—sometimes "in your face" and noisy, other times and places done in privacy and quiet, forceful and aggressive in a different way. Some cultures have negotiation rituals that must be observed.

Each culture and many subcultures have unwritten rules about how to negotiate, and what about. We are aware that our new system will serve cultures within communities, and that this idea may be important as to preferences about dispute resolution systems.

Mediation

Conciliation and negotiation are the clear preference of humans, worldwide, for resolving their disputes. Humans don't like to have a third person intervene.

A very, very long time ago, people realized that conciliation and negotiation did not resolve every dispute. Our ancestors resorted to magic, religion, combat, and complex (though reasoned) procedures provided by governments to resolve disputes over thousands of years.

Sometimes it was necessary to let a third person help resolve the dispute. Even today, people don't like the third person to make a decision for them. They prefer, if a third person is to be involved, that the person be a mediator. Mediators help the disputants make a decision. Mediators don't make decisions for the disputants then impose their will upon the disputants.

Humans must have always informally and instinctively relied on mediation when they could not work things out for themselves.

Mediation brought a third person to the dispute, but not to act as a judge or decision maker. The third person's task was to enhance and assist the negotiations between disputants. The third person would listen, evaluate, make suggestions, encourage movement, cajole, point out weaknesses in each position, maybe even caution the disputers about possible dire results if the matter were not resolved.

Mediators often force disputants to face the necessity of resort to government decision makers should they fail to make a decision of their own.

It isn't that we prefer mediation. Rather, we prefer it to any other way of bringing a third person into a dispute. Clearly, people worldwide don't want to let a third party make an enforceable decision about a dispute. All of the world's governments use forms of trials, with government officials making decisions about disputes brought before them. All of the world's people know that letting the government decide and enforce its decision is the least desirable way of handling disputes.

I should give credit to Allen Lind, Ph.D., for his research into our preferences for methods of dispute resolution. Lind's research revealed that all ethnic groups preferred to settle disputes one-on-one. When they couldn't, they wanted a mediator to help. If that didn't work, they would grudgingly accept the decision of a third party adjudicator…a judge or arbitrator.

Adjudication

All of the world's methods of dispute resolution other than conciliation, negotiation, and mediation are more complicated. As a result, we note a major distinction.

In conciliation and mediation, the disputants are in control. They do most of the talking and do not need the help of any of the attorney classes to assist them. Attorneys might be invited to attend, as they are helpful resources.

In progressing through the list of the adjudication processes that follow, the people who own the dispute have increasingly minor roles. Typically, roles limited to answering questions asked by an attorney practically required to represent disputants in these other, more complicated processes.

In advisory arbitration proceedings (in which the decision, or "award," is not binding upon the disputants); disputants are freer to talk.

There are many variations on the theme when the third party makes a decision for the people who own the dispute. They can be cataloged as follows.

Adjudication by Agreement "Arbitration"

The disputants, in desperation to end their dispute and the costs of continuing it, agree upon a mutually respected third person to decide the dispute for them. This work is done without government involvement, although the award may be enforced by government courts if not voluntarily complied with by either party.

In some forms of arbitration a third party or organization chooses the arbitrator for the disputants. Many disputants report dissatisfaction with the process, and regret not having chosen an arbitrator before the dispute erupted.

Three major classes of arbitration have emerged. Advisory, "penalty arbitration," and binding arbitration.

All three forms physically proceed much as adversary trials. They are relatively less formal and have fewer "rules of procedure" and "rules of evidence," but since they are conducted by agreements of the disputants, the disputants may agree to make them as complicated as they chose.

Advisory Arbitration

Advisory arbitration is like a trial, with each side presenting "evidence" and the arguments of their counsel. However, the decision made by the third party cannot be enforced against any disputant. Disputants either comply, continue to negotiate, or refuse to comply. If they refuse, the other side will likely go to the government's courts for a trial. Disputants usually agree, in advance of the arbitration, that the arbitrator's decision will not be revealed to government judges and juries.

Penalty Arbitration

As with advisory arbitration, the award in penalty arbitration is not enforceable against the loser. However, should the loser refuse to comply with the award, the parties are required to proceed to government courts for a decision through trial, but only by taking on increased risk. If the party asking for the trial does not obtain a better result in court than that awarded by the arbitrator, that party is required to pay the legal fees and costs for the winner. These fees are calculated from the time of arbitration award through the end of the government trial.

The fearful uncertainty of the outcome of government trials causes most losers to accept the award or negotiate to a settlement based on the award.

Binding Arbitration

The third form of arbitration results in an award that may be transformed into a government-enforced judgment, if not complied with by the loser. This form of arbitration is most like a government trial. Because of the difficulty with conducting these arbitrations, they are typically conducted by lawyers. The role of the disputants is limited to answering attorneys, and sometimes arbitrators' questions. There is no appeal from these awards, although government judges will set them aside if there is fraud or any other serious defect in the way the proceedings were conducted or the award procured. Government judges were once jealous of private arbitrators and had sometimes set their awards aside, but as government courts became overloaded with disputes, judges seldom set awards aside. Even when the award might seem "arbitrary" and not based on local law!

Trials

Most governments call their dispute resolution processes "trials." Few governments offer formal mediation. Cultures differ and governments have different histories. This leads to variations in the ways governments "try" cases and resolve disputes.

There are "adversary" trials and "inquisitorial" trials. The inquisitorial method of trying lawsuits is in no significant way related to the Spanish "Inquisition" of centuries past. That institution resulted in many injustices based on little more than a person's religious beliefs. The inquisitorial method of trials permits the decision maker to ask questions and to investigate. Governments that offer only adversary trials make an additional distinction between matters decided by judges alone and those decided by citizen juries.

The decision may be made by a "jury" of people temporarily employed by the courts (at very low fees, and without any real option to decline the opportunity to serve), or by a "judge." The jury's decisions are always subject to review by one or more judges who might disagree with the jury's decision and set it aside.

Adversary Trials

The principle distinction between adversary trials and inquisitorial trials stems from the role of the government judge.

In Adversarial Trials, the judge is expected to conduct the proceedings according to pre-established rules. The judge is a passive participant as evidence is presented by disputants, except for speaking about purely procedural matters ("time for lunch!") or ruling on legal issues when requested by one of the lawyers who really run the trial ("Your honor, I object." "Overruled!").

These judges are not permitted to suggest what issues should be decided or what evidence should be brought to the trials. They are forbidden to argue for a particular outcome. Only when the lawyers have had their say, and "rested," does the judge make a decision about the outcome or "instruct" the jury about the law they should apply in arriving at their decision. The judge is forbidden to investigate the case or call a witness of their own.

There are some exceptions. Some American governments permit adversarial judges to have social workers look into the welfare of children of dissolving marriages, for example.

When an adversarial trial system employs jurors, they make the decision about the case. In these trials, adversarial judges were warned to be even more passive, as they might "bias" the jury by some remark or action.

Inquisitorial Trials

The inquisitorial trial uses attorneys, as does the adversarial system, but the judge's role is that of investigator and analyst as well as procedural guardian and decision maker. These are "three-cornered" trials, with the judge taking a much more active role than an adversarial judge.

The Inquisitorial trial is less "game-like" than the adversarial trial. The inquisitorial judge might remind the attorney of a missing essential and permit the attorney time to find and provide the missing information. Adversary trials let each attorney take advantage of the oversights and mistakes of the other, even to the point of allowing loss of a case over a technical point. Adversary trials are widely touted by the attorneys and judges as "a search for the truth," despite their trickiness.

Attorneys in adversary systems dislike the concept of the inquisitorial trial. They see the inquisitorial method as an unwarranted intrusion into their powers of control over cases. They all seem to think that only the other lawyer will make a fateful mistake, damning his client to an unjust outcome.

Appeals

No government court review of the way an arbitration is handled is possible, except in cases such as the bribery of the arbitrator or some similar, fundamental problem of misconduct.

Both adversary and inquisitorial government trial processes allow appeals.

Usually, there is only one disputant believing they have been wronged by the government decision maker. Often enough, though, both disputants think they have been wronged. Judges are heard to say, "If both sides are upset with the decision, it must have been right!" Most of the rest of us are very suspicious of this idea.

An appeal may be taken by a disputant who thinks the answer from the trial was wrong, but taking an appeal isn't like getting to try the case all over again. Taking an appeal means only that a set of more highly compensated judges will review whether the trial judge had correctly understood and applied the "law."

Governments don't want the rules to change too rapidly. The appellate judges are expected to keep things in line. Appeals take a long time, and the results of trials are seldom changed. However, they sometimes are a source of change. That they might be the source of change is always a source of lively controversy in countries contemplating the fact that popularly elected legislative bodies should be the source of changes.

Executive Branches of Government

Many governments (perhaps most) observe a functional and legal distinction between the "judicial" branch and the "executive" branch. Quite a few add another branch, called the "legislative" branch. Here's how they work, and how these other branches got into providing dispute resolution to citizens.

Historically, humanity's first governments did it all. The chief, king or emperor made laws (the legislative function), pursued possible violators (the executive function) decided when they had been violated, or should be enforced (the judicial function), then enforced them with police, armies or the castle guards (the executive function).

Later, as populations grew, these jobs were delegated. Sometimes the legislative function was torn from the leader by revolution. It was then said to belong "to the people," although many of the people confessed that they doubted this was really so.

The executive function might be discharged by an individual or a committee, but it always sought more power and influence. Thus began a practice of "administrative hearings." These were almost always conducted by the attorney class, originally trained to serve the judicial branch. Executives, being no fools, knew they were creating a parallel to the Judicial when they persuaded the legislative branches (when there was one) to let them create "administrative law."

Administrative courts disturb many thoughtful people. They worry that executives create rules (administrative law, such as tax regulations) which were thought to be a legislative function. They worry more, as the executives create their own courts (a judicial function), to decide if they had been right to charge a citizen with an infraction of the rules. In our country, one such executive court is the Internal Revenue Service's own "Tax Court." Then, if the executive courts find the citizen in the wrong, the executive branch enforces the decision against the citizen. This latter step seems the only legitimate act performed in the entire process.

Well-financed interests use the legislative and executive branches to make decisions the judicial branch would not, or could not make. Disputes are resolved by passing laws (a legislative function) or by creating an administrative rule or regulation (another legislative function). "Lobbying" is the process of persuading these branches of government to make a decision resolving the dispute, perhaps because those hired to persuade the government hang around a lot in lobbies, waiting on their targets to appear?

International Organizations

Organizations of countries make efforts to resolve conflict when collisions of national interests occur. These bodies seldom have the power to intervene in the affairs of wealthy countries, but they often intervene in the internal affairs of less wealthy disputants.

There are also international organizations providing dispute resolution services to international commerce. A current trend seems to lean toward using mediation and arbitration as the primary means of resolution. Logical, in view of the preference of all human cultures for mediated settlements when negotiation fails.

Combat

Amazingly, we people still fight, physically, to end some disputes. Usually, these disputes are between governments, driven by economic concerns.

It is increasingly harder for governments to convince ordinary citizens that war is a bright and good thing to do. We have to be convinced that the "enemy" government will steal more from us than will the government with which we live. Lacking this conviction, citizens more often find themselves in conflict with governments, leading to increased use of the government's courts.

Summary

In most of the countries of the world, governments provide trials as a proxy for physical combat. Many other countries have cultures which provide alternatives to use of the trial system. The U. S. culture does not.

As we have grown more populous, waning attention to management of interpersonal and organizational disputes has resulted in atrophy of fundamental dispute resolution techniques.

Governments and those who profit from use of government facilities choose methods that preserve their power, and their incomes. There is widespread dissatisfaction with the ways governments provide dispute resolution to us, yet we have not become willing to take responsibility for the ways our disputes are resolved. We continue to delegate this vital function to the bureaucracies and to the lawyers.

4

How We Got This Way—Leaving it to "The Government"

The *adversary* trial method is the dominant pervasive method of dispute resolution provided by governments through the courts and through administrative hearings in the United States. Even though administrative hearings (such as zoning issues, quarrels over permits to use land) are not called "trials," the procedural method used to resolve these disputes is the *adversary* method.

The adversary method assumes the presence of one or more decision makers. Depending on the type of case, legal tradition will let a judge alone decide the case, or he will dictate that a jury decide it. In theory, the decision makers in adversary proceedings are passive listeners who do not ask questions, suggest issues or investigate any assertion of the disputants. Once the disputants have finished presentation of their "evidence" and "arguments," the third party or parties will consider, then articulate, their decision. They are not usually required to give reasons for the decision they have made.

When using the adversary method, the adversaries make decisions about what issues should be decided and what information should be given to the decision maker. The judge or jury is only permitted to decide issues submitted by the adversaries.

Adversary trial judges may, with limitations, ignore the decisions of juries, and may, within limits, even modify them.

Inquisitorial trials differ from adversarial trials. Inquisitorial systems permit the decision maker to raise issues and to investigate and provide evidence in addition to that produced by the adversaries. Probably more countries use inquisitorial trial methods than adversarial trial methods. This is not to argue that they are better, only different. Inquisitorial systems concentrate power on the judges; adversarial systems concentrate power on the attorneys.

In an effort to limit the power of the judiciary, Americans have chosen the adversary model. We have only been partly successful in our choice, as federal judges seem more inclined to the three-cornered trials of the inquisitorial courts. State trial judges, elected periodically, hew to the adversary model with greater purity.

So! How did we come to handle public dispute resolution as we do? The story begins in the British isles, long ago.

When the ancient Normans invaded England, they wanted to steal the land, dominate the people and live off the spoils. They succeeded.

They knew that they must not permit independent institutions to resolve significant disputes—not disputes among themselves or disputes among the governed.

Even Magna Carta preserved the existing central and powerful system of control over the resolution of disputes. In that document, King John gave up some powers of dispute resolution to the barons who faced him down at Runnymede Meadow. Magna Carta was not about little peoples' rights; it was about the rights of barons.

Today we refer to our governmental system of dispute resolution as "Court." The origins of the word are embarrassingly obvious. The Norman kings and dukes provided dispute resolution through their "courts," as did the islands' rulers before them.

Attendance at court and an audience with the local royalty or baron were essential to power-backed resolution of private disputes. An enforceable resolution was required when an adversary did not live up to a bargain or refused to negotiate an end to a dispute. The only forum for enforceable, legal resolution was either the king's or his dele-gates' "court."

Because of other interests and the pressing need to keep power over their subjects, the Normans delegated some of the business of resolving private disputes to trusted others. The others were members of court. These were "royals," or nearly so, who dispensed with justice or dis-pensed justice as they were disposed. In the morning, sword practice or caring for the horses. In the afternoon, a civil or criminal trial.

Over time, the English gravitated toward letting locals decide local issues. At first the jury consisted of people who were familiar with the problem; people we would today classify as "witnesses" were then the jurors. The inheritors of the Norman principle were not yet ready to lose their grasp on how citizens should resolve their disputes. Should the local lord disagree with the locals' decision, they simply imposed their own decision, and to hell with the locals!

Later, political pressures caused Parliament and the English judges by now no longer members of aristocratic courts—to increasingly give decision making power to juries. Members of juries no longer had to be knowledgeable, and by now were selected in the main for their igno-rance of what had happened.

The last great case in which an English judge attempted to force jurors to his view involved the trial of some of William Penn's follow-ers. The judge disliked the first verdict of the jury and had the jury locked up in the Tower of London until they returned a verdict more to his liking! The House of Lords, the last remnant of royal power over private dispute resolution and then the only appeal from such deci-sions, held that a judge must accept a jury's decision in such matters, even though the judge disagreed with the jury.

Had the Norman aristocracy of England relinquished control over the dispute resolution *process?* Hardly so! Through political control of Parliament and powerful influence over who might be appointed to the bench, control remained in the rulers. To this day, control of

England's courts remains in the hands of the English upper economic classes.

So what happened in America?

Please recall that in revolutionary times there was no economic middle class. There were wealthy people: aristocrats, landowners and merchants—and those they employed or used. This condition existed in the Eastern United States until the nineteenth century.

Rulers have never perceived it to be to their advantage to delegate dispute resolution entirely to the people. State control, and in turn control of the State, has been the goal of those who have power.

As wealthy and powerful interests in America devised the way in which the United States was to be organized, an interesting anomaly was created and preserved. In a country that emphasized independence, individuality and control of the government by the people, the powerful crafted a system that, in a limited way preserved the aristocratic English idea of royalty. We elect only our congress directly. The "Electoral College," not the voters, selects the president.. More importantly to our discussions, our founders adopted a scheme that continued to deprive us of the right to control how our disputes are resolved, and by whom. Our founders created the federal judiciary.

Our federal "court" is a reflection of the aristocratic English court of revolutionary times. Its members are to this day appointed for life. The Congress alone can act to remove them. Access to them was and is unavailable to "the people," except in formal proceedings resulting from filing lawsuits. They were and are appointed by a person not directly or popularly elected, subject only to a veto by popularly elected senators. Only impeachment can remove them from office. Only two have been impeached in the over two hundred years of our history as the United States of America. As was true for the Norman Kings, the power of our federal judges over citizens is subject only to the most limited review. Alexis de Tocqueville observed that the United States' federal judges were the last vestige of royalty—the only princes in America, secure for their lives in their jobs, and in their compensation.

John Marshall, our first Chief Justice, is credited with authoring the doctrine of "separation of powers." It was crafted for the ostensible purpose of assuring that neither the executive nor legislative branches of the federal government would be all-powerful. Incidentally, it ensured enormous power to the federal judiciary. It made the third branch of government the final editing power for all that the executive or legislative branches might attempt. Early in our country's history, the princes of the American judicial system used cases which were appealed to them to reserve power to themselves to conceptualize and actualize the system of dispute resolution upon which most Americans depended. They kept for themselves the power of the Norman Kings.

The Norman Kings could speedily remove their judges. The American system cannot. The result has been stagnation among the appointed-for-life. Too many of them have little motivation to act powerfully and decisively to assure the growth of the system and its adaptation to its changing environment.

No less so than their English predecessors, American judges realized the plenary power over community life which their federal sinecures delivered. Our federal judges are lifetime aristocrats. Royalty for life, and untouchables, we accept the good their lifetime sinecures permit them to do and resent that which we perceive as evil.

The reaction of the people to this aspect of the federal constitutional design has been evident. Jeffersonian and Jacksonian ideas resulted in few states adopting appointive judges that were also difficult to remove. Jackson's followers, notably in the southern and western states, chose elected judges, permitting them relatively short terms between elections. Wealthy people crafted the United States Constitution, less wealthy people the constitutions of the States. The difference shows.

Today we see the impetus for change coming from the states, not from the federal judicial system. There should be no surprise in this when we recognize the origins and purpose of the federal system. It is designed and implemented to preserve the status quo.

State systems *tend* to the status quo, but because their judges are elected, there is increased responsiveness to the wishes of the people as expressed through legislative bodies.

Witness the Florida experience. Although the Florida courts could readily have modified the system to depart from the ancient English model, the impetus for change came from the legislature of the state. That body was far more sensitive to the mood of an unhappy public that wished for a change. Once Florida's legislature took the lead, the courts obligingly followed.

What have court systems done to improve their services? How have lawyers and judges coped with the demands of the public they serve?

We have indeed come a long way! The early English courts were content to let criminal and civil disputes be decided by combat and physical contests. Later, they were decided by ordeals such as immersing the arm of an accused person in boiling water or oil. Did the arm infect in a week or so? Then the accused was guilty. Still later, it was done by oath-taking. By correctly repeating a lengthy oath, a person might win a case. Miss a word or stutter and you lost.

Since then, less dramatic but important changes have come along.

At first, and since, courts have been preoccupied with finding what the "truth" might be. When the metaphysical bases of trial by combat, ordeal and oath fell on hard times, courts looked to the new rationalism for means of determining the truth.

From time to time people have believed that juries could decide what the truth might be. We are constantly reminded of the frailty of that assumption. Lawyers and judges are members of their cultures. They should be forgiven for sharing the fallacious belief that once on a jury, a citizen would transcend the limitations of human cognitive and perceptual capacities and "find" the truth that had eluded the disputing parties, hence an unwarranted trust of the jury trial system.

In America the jury trial seemed consistent with our other assumptions about people governing themselves. Jacksonian and Jeffersonian alike heralded the jury trial as a means of buffering between governments and citizens.

A closer look at the *adversary* jury trial system shows the deceptions that were, and are practiced on casual consumers of its products.

How are juries "selected"? They aren't. The "jury" is a collection of people left after the adversaries have excluded those perceived to be most biased in favor of the other side of the contest. The jury is a residue—a distillate.

The information given to a jury clearly influences its decision. What information is a jury permitted to hear in order to do its work?

Adversary trials are designed to *limit* the amount of information a jury receives. Rules of evidence are used to eliminate information from the jury's hearing and sight. An example of such a rule is the "hearsay" rule. We all know that serial communication—what she says he says they said…is unreliable. The hearsay rule makes that a matter of law. Jurors are not allowed to know of this information. The jury doesn't evaluate the reliability of the information; the judge does.

Aristocratic, class-conscious English judges crafted the first "rules of evidence." American judges and legislatures have added to them and modified them. The legal assumption that ordinary people cannot be trusted to correctly evaluate the importance of information or its reliability is the reason for the rules of evidence. Confessions are excluded in criminal trials, copies of documents in civil cases, and information about suspicions and beliefs in divorce cases. Opinions about the evidence may only be voiced by "experts."

Not only is the information given to juries partial and incomplete, but juries don't know that they are getting less than the full story. Jurors are permitted to ask only the most perfunctory questions. If they go beyond those, they receive answers from the judge such as, "The answer will be found in the evidence which you find to be reliable."

Jurors in most states and in most trials are not allowed to take notes. This rule stems from a time when few people were literate. Jurists believed that a note taker might dominate the minds of lesser persons on the jury. The rule is no longer based on a viable reason, but that seems a small concern for those who manage the adversary trial system.

Jury instructions are the means by which jurors are expected to learn what the job is and what they should have been listening for. We don't tell jurors what to listen and look for until the trial is over! The judges "instructions to the jury" are read to them at the *end* of the trial. Worse still, the instructions are a collection of abstraction statements made in elegant, often archaic language. The instructions do not tell the jury succinctly what to decide or in what order the issues are to be decided. To top it off, few states in only a few kinds of trials give the jurors copies of the instructions to read and use while deliberating their decision.

So how is it that juries are to "find the truth"? We don't tell them the whole story, do not let them take notes, refuse to let them ask questions, and do not describe the job to them until the trial is over. Can you now understand why juries so often reach results you find inconsistent with the information you have been given firsthand or by the media? The information you received was unrestricted by "rules of evidence" and the practices of trial lawyers and judges. You were permitted to ask questions, take notes if you wished, and to demand answers.

Although infatuated with ideas about how to conduct a "search for the truth," lawyers, judges and legal scholars have explored other fixes for the adversary trial method.

At an earlier time, and up until this century, many believed that the answer to a better system might lie in perfecting the communication between lawyers and between lawyers and judges. They began to refine the system of "pleading." The end result was to virtually try the case on paper. If the magic words were written, the other side might capitulate. The papers filed by lawyers contained their version of "the truth." The other side rarely saw this as a reliable source.

The papers filed in court became too voluminous and increasingly unreliable. Another path to the truth had to be found.

"Discovery" was the twentieth century fix. Two issues were resolved. First, that the initial papers filed only needed to vaguely advise the opponent of the nature of the claim or defenses to it; second, that lawyers should turn to digging for *information* from the other side. Judges were empowered to force the disclosure of information, except when the information was protected by law. Judges could and can be relied upon to force disclosures of all sorts of information, *even knowing it will and can never be used in court because of the way the rules of evidence work*!

The principle energies of lawyers charged with resolving a dispute through the adversary trial now began to get as much information as possible from the opponent. Not incidentally, lawyers sought information that required punitive levels of effort from an opponent. Discovery "abuses" became a topic of legal writing and concern in the seventies, eighties and nineties of our century.

So whither now with the adversary trial? The latest attempt to make it work is to force "voluntary disclosures." Significant penalties will apply to those who fail to "voluntarily" disclose pertinent information. Even now, only a few years after adoption of the new concept, it seems to be inadequate. Many lawyers feel the idea is a failure.

A fundamental error of approach and thinking is the source of our professional and personal frustration with the contemporary judicial system. We have tried to make one method—the adversary trial—resolve all disputes. We ask it to satisfy the needs of all disputants while satisfying community needs for resolution of disputes in a generally acceptable way.

We should now recognize that one method cannot do all this. The answer lies in providing multiple methods and redundant paths to dispute resolution. It lies as well in taking private, personal, and corporate responsibility for our disputes and in delegating very few disputes to public dispute resolution.

We must end our heavy dependency on lawyers and judges and on the judicial system for resolving problems we can and should resolve for ourselves.

The courts and lawyers can no longer be the answer to all our problems. We must shake our traditional acceptance of, and reliance upon a system descended from monarchs and nobles. We need to recall our roots.

How would Jefferson and Jackson design a system, faced with our troubled times? Upon what would they rely, given our much broader and deeper knowledge of humanity and how humans work and play?

Imagine a clean slate upon which to write a court system for our times, with no need to copy the institutions of the past, with no need to serve the interests of the powerful. Armed with the knowledge of humanity and humans which we have today, and given the working power of our marvelous, emerging technologies, what would you design? How would it work, and whom would it serve?

5

What Can We Do As Individuals, Businesses and Governments?

Do we use the adversary trial in our *new* system?

If we do not use the adversary method, we will lose the advantages it offers for certain kinds of disputes.

It is slow and deliberate. We know there are complex and worrisome matters that should be approached slowly and deliberately about which we should accumulate volumes of information before a decision is attempted. It creates precedents that guide us in planning for the future and in adjusting to social change. Sometimes the legislative branch fails to do so. The courts can be a moral force when the other branches of government seem powerless to act.

We retain the adversary method, but we recognize that it cannot stand alone as the government's only offering for resolving our disputes.

Is there a hidden requirement, not articulated in our Constitution, that the government's courts may use only one method? There is not. It's just the way we've always done it.

Does our bottle cure *some* problems? Is the adversary trial necessary for some of our constitutional ideas to work at all? If so, we shouldn't junk it. What do we do about the problems its use *creates*, and those disputes that don't respond well to this method?

There is an old woodsman's statement that can help us. "When you aren't sure which way to go, sit down."

Sit with me for a moment. The first task is to forget where we've been, but only for the time it takes to read this chapter. We cannot permanently abandon our history or the resources it provides or the momentum with which it propels us.

The second task is to wipe your mental slate clean. Pretend, for the moments you are reading this chapter, that there has never before been a need for courts or a need to resolve disputes among humans.

Next, assume that suddenly all the kinds of disputes we know have erupted. You and I will provide an answer for the nation's problem.

We have at our command all the accumulated knowledge of individual and organizational behavior that our researchers and universities can provide. We have been granted the power and funds to implement the solutions we believe will meet the sudden, new demands of our national community.

I know this next fantasy will be the toughest one for you, but try. Imagine that Congress won't tinker with our solution!

We know it is better to plan before we act. Furniture makers working with rare woods know the wisdom of the homily, "Measure twice, cut once." We believe that the solutions we provide must work well from the beginning. The need to be right the first time is great. Our neighbors tell us the methods used by our neighbor nations are "too expensive, too slow, and too complicated." Our community needs relief immediately.

First, we list our goals. They are:

The system will move adequate numbers of cases to resolution

The system will resolve cases quickly

The system will be simple enough that most people can use it without special assistance, for the greatest possible numbers of cases

The system will emphasize redundancy of path and variety of method for dispute resolution

The system will move each case to the most appropriate dispute resolution path—to the simplest method likely to be effective for the dispute and its owners

The system will permit cases of possible social concern or precedential value to be identified and considered differently

The system will encourage and support the establishment of private dispute resolution: interpersonal, intra-organization and inter-organization

The system will move cases that can be handled privately into private dispute resolution and out of government channels

The system will, wherever feasible and to the extent possible, collect its cost from users

The system will gain feedback from consumers, the public, its providers and its managers

The system will continually self adjust, based on management's responses to information systems designed to assure dynamism and growth

The costs of the system will remain proportionate to its continuing benefits, as benefits are perceived by consumers, public, providers and managers

Our criteria in mind, we plan the chronological order of the work that will have to do to conceptualize and implement the new system:

Present and possible future consumers of dispute resolution services will be identified

Demographic characteristics of populations of consumers will be related to the types of disputes of which they complain

Processes for dispute resolution worldwide will be identified and catalogued

Processes responding to consumer needs and demographics will be chosen

How much of the work can be done privately, how much must be performed by government?

The process array will be established

Rules for both substantive and procedural aspects will be drafted and adopted

Management information systems will be designed and tested to assure adequate and continuous feedback of efficiency and attitudinal data to system managers

Management methods will be implemented to assure continuous and immediate correction within the system, as near as possible to the points of service delivery

Communication will be planned for system wide access to information about performance, modifications and needs.

Staffing begins

We will choose process managers

We will choose service providers

Training begins

We will train process managers

We will train service providers

Consumers will be informed about the system and intake will begin

Feedback and response will begin at the management level

Fine tuning begins—and never ends

Public, consumer, provider and management satisfaction measurement begins—and never ends

Fine tuning and modification is the continuous response of the system to management data it generates

Having progressed to this point, we are relieved that we haven't designed just a project, but have conceptualized a system. One of the hallmarks of a system is that its work is never done. It evolves, learning from the senses we have given it about its environment and its capacities. A system expects to be modified, to grow and change, to find means for responding to the humans who give it life and vitality. A system is never a finished work.

Finally, we must design and articulate the criteria by which we will know, at any time, if our system is healthy and functioning as we designed it.

Our first step will be to totally abandon one of the subtle precepts upon which our ancient system of adversary trials is based. The precept is that if the system is perfect as an abstraction, it is perfect in reality. If such thinking were true, finished buildings would be exactly as planned!

Consumer, public, provider and manager satisfaction are of very little concern to the judicial nobles who own and operate the American justice system. When were you last asked if the courts were operating to your satisfaction? If you were asked, I'll bet it was not by a lawyer or a judge, eager to make the system responsive to your needs.

The proposition that the system need satisfy only the legal abstractions of "justice" and "fairness" is the source of this lack of concern. "If the result is in compliance with law, it *is* fair and just," according to the bench and legal profession. My attitudes and yours are irrelevant if we accept this standard.

At its worst, this is the proposition that permits, even causes lawyers and judges to defend the acquittal of persons who have confessed their guilt, when their confessions are "suppressed" because of the hint of a promise of different treatment if they will tell all. Juries, deprived of this information, acquit.

A deeper, more ominous reason for the present system's lack of care for others' attitudes about the system lies in power's bed. Power over governmental systems for dispute resolution is unique. Judges and justices make laws daily. Some apply nationally. Other such laws apply only to the litigants. Their "opinions" and rulings are enforced with the power of the executive branch. Only legislation can thwart them—at times only constitutional amendment. Voters find it virtually impossible to remove a federal judge or justice. State court judges, although elected, are very difficult to beat at the polls.

Our new system must be responsive to public perceptions of satisfactory operation. The first criterion for our system will be that these groups will on an ongoing basis find the system satisfactory:

> Consumers of services—those that go to court, whether as civil litigants, victims of crimes, or as accused persons. (We acknowledge that the weight to be given the attitudes of accused persons later convicted will have to be adjusted for.)

> The public—Are results coming from the system in keeping with the peoples' ideas about how disputes should be managed and what results should occur in broad classes of disputes?

> Service providers—Is the system adequately supporting them? Do they perceive their work as appropriate and necessary?

> System managers—is the system adequately informing them and is it adequately responsive to them?

In the next chapter we'll discuss how the new American system might look.

6

Using Dispute Management Principles to Improve a State Court System

The late sixties and early seventies were times of reexamination for many Americans. In my thirties, I was deeply disturbed by the shortcomings of our legal system. I began the research and thinking that led to the set of methods and principles that I named "Dispute Management."

I wrote my first monograph about better dispute resolution in 1972. In it, I argued that Florida's response to a dissolving marriage should be mediation, not litigation. The state's courts should send divorcing couples to trained mediators. These people would aid them in resolving their disputes and see to it that the children's interests were respected. The mediators would provide them with guidance through the paperwork and procedural maze of the court system.

I then believed that not less than eighty-five percent of all contested family cases could be resolved without the necessity of an adversary process. It seemed silly to me that a spouse should have to hire lawyers and sue their mate before being assisted in negotiating a settlement. Even then, virtually all family suits ended by settlement. If most cases were going to be resolved by settlement negotiations, why not choose a process that enhanced negotiation potentials? Mediation seemed such a logical choice, as opposed to an adversary trial process.

The naive might assume from state court statistics that trials must occur in all family cases, or else how would a judgment of divorce have been entered? Judges *rubber stamp* the couples' decisions with a "Final Judgment." There is only rarely a trial—outcomes are negotiated.

I thought we should alter the system to fit the reality. An adversary process simply was not required, or even helpful in these cases. The few cases that needed a decision maker could still have them, but the system should be designed for the huge majority of cases, not the few aberrations!

Part of the reality of 1972 was an entrenched family law bar and bench, making good livings from the status quo.[1] Once you were married, you would use their system, *or you could not end your marriage.* Hardly a thought on wedding days, but a bitter reality for many couples only years later.

I had written a piece for which there seemed no audience. The idea of using a mediator instead of a judge and mediation instead of adversary trials and lawyers was too far ahead of its time. Or, I optimistically thought, I simply had been among the first to propose it. I could not find a publisher for the monograph. Happily, sixteen years from reading it, one of its first readers saw to it that a bill passed Florida's legislature, making mediation and two forms of arbitration part of the Florida court system.[2]

The Legislative Study Commission On Alternative Dispute Resolution for the Courts had generated the bill. Florida's Legislature created the Commission. I was appointed to it, and elected Chair. It was the opportunity I had begun preparing for as a dissatisfied young attorney in the sixties.

---

1.   This resistance to quicker, simpler and less expensive means of resolving family disputes continues to this day. Colorado lawyers are required to advise new clients of the availability of alternative methods of dispute resolution, and their relative cost. Other states have yet to require family lawyers to "tell all." As long as it is in lawyers' financial interests to obscure and delay, even ignore better methods of dispute resolution, altogether too many of them will not inform their clients candidly about these processes.

2.   Senator Helen Gordon Davis, of Tampa, guided the bill through to adoption in Florida's 1987 legislative session.

In the years following my first monograph, I consumed whatever information I could find concerning means of dispute resolution. The "alternative" culture of the late sixties and early seventies adopted mediation as preferred over the offering of governments' courts. I learned that mediation was only one of many engines, and that none of them would prove useful unless placed in a frame, with controls provided for users.

I began to think in terms of dispute *management*, not dispute *resolution*. Mediation, arbitration and trials would resolve disputes, but it was the management of the populations of disputes that needed attention. These processes needed to be considered as parts of *systems*.

In 1987, Florida's legislature passed the revolutionary legislation offered by the commission I had been so fortunate to chair. The legislation was the first expression of what might happen in a system if Dispute Management principles were applied. The "engines" were now in place in a frame.

Within a few weeks of passage of the bill, the Honorable Parker Lee McDonald, Chief Justice of Florida's Supreme Court, appointed me to chair a newly created Mediation and Arbitration Rules Committee. In January of 1988 I presented my Committee's draft of the Rules of Procedure designed to give access to the new newly added processes. It was during this presentation to The Supreme Court of Florida that I first publicly articulated the basic criteria for a Dispute Management approach to conflict resolution in the courts.[3]

The "engines" were now in the frame, with controls in place. The first court system altered by application of Dispute Management principles would soon begin to operate.

Sixteen years had passed since I had first proposed a system that would manage disputes in a different way. Florida's Supreme Court unanimously approved the proposed rules, to my joy and relief.

---

3.   The proceedings were videotaped, and copies are available from the Dispute Resolution Center, Office of the State Courts Administrator, Supreme Court Building, Tallahassee, Florida.

When Dispute management principles were applied to the Florida Court system, they revealed the principle weaknesses of all American court systems—state and federal. To spotlight the system's weaknesses, let's apply those principles.

First, we should review the principles discussed more fully in Chapter 2. These are criteria by which we may judge the existing system, and any ideas for change.

Initially, we will consider the existing system. We don't want to throw out anything that is working. To determine what should be retained, we will apply the Dispute Management system objectives, then we will apply the Dispute Management order of work to show what steps should be taken in deciding how to modify the system. To conclude, we will again apply the Dispute Management principles to demonstrate *how* the new system was implemented, and how it is working.

The system will move adequate numbers of cases to resolution

Backlogs of cases were only beginning to surface as a problem in the early '80's, and only in urban areas, but Florida was now the nation's fourth largest state, and still growing. Thoughtful leaders realized that the rates of case filing increase exponentially with population increase and increased density of populations. Lawyer advertising was to become a factor in increased awareness about the ease of access to the courts. Florida could look to California and New York to see jurisdictions reporting five to seven years' backlog of cases. The Florida judicial system was too much like the systems of those states to avoid the same future.

The system will resolve cases quickly

The key to backlog avoidance is quick handling of cases. Lawyers in Florida were generally satisfied with the year to two years it took to process litigated matters. They were frustrated with slower handling in some areas of the state. No one thought cases could be handled more quickly because no one thought the adversary process should be abandoned. The process is *designed* to be slow and deliberate.

The system will be simple enough that most people can use it without special assistance, for the greatest possible numbers of cases

Florida's courts relied entirely on one process for handling all cases brought to it. Adversary hearings and trials were the only cures for lawsuits, and the disputes that caused them. Three years of law school is barely a start in understanding how the adversary court system operates. Most lawyers agree that they didn't mature in their sophistication about the system until five to seven years after being admitted to the bar. Non-lawyers cannot effectively use the system and there is no quick way to teach them about handling a dispute through adversary processes. A wrong move and your case is lost. The good news about adversary processes is the very thoroughness that makes them so complicated and slow. The process can accumulate volumes of information about a subject. If the matter is of social importance, such as the question of segregated schooling, vans will be required to move the physical case files from point to point. When a deep probe is warranted and when the information about a case may be as important as its final disposition, adversary processes are desirable.

The system will emphasize redundancy of path and variety of method for dispute resolution

Florida's courts relied only on an adversary method. There was no other path and no other method for resolving disputes in court.

The system will move each case to the most appropriate dispute resolution path—to the simplest method likely to be effective for the dispute and its owners

Without redundancy of path and variety of method, this can't be done. Florida had neither.

The system will permit cases of possible social concern or precedential value to be identified and considered differently

All cases were treated the same. Special attention was granted only for the rarely used common law writs and for very few social issues, such as the emergency interests of children in a dissolving marriage.

The system will encourage and support the establishment of private dispute resolution—interpersonal, intra-organization and inter-organization

In an indirect way, the system's reliance on only adversary process was encouraging the move to private dispute resolution. Some judges had begun to lean heavily on litigators to use the services of private mediators. The mediators were successful in ending about seventy percent of the disputes thus "referred" to them.

In several areas of the state there were local mediation programs devoted only to post-judgment disputes in divorce cases or to small claims in county courts, but these efforts were not system wide. They were symptoms of the growing problem with efficient case handling, and not a systemic cure.

The system will move cases that can be handled privately into private dispute resolution and out of government channels

See above.

The system will, wherever feasible and to the extent possible, collect its cost from users

Although Florida's judges had scant authority to do so, those that "encouraged" counsel to take cases to private mediators also set the fees for the mediators. The judges had no budget from which to pay for the mediation sessions they wanted to occur. Out of necessity they invented "toll road justice." Lawyers and their clients paid the tolls, initially out of fear or respect for the judges' wishes.

The system will gain feedback from consumers, the public, its providers, and its managers

Florida's system received only limited informal attitudinal feedback from lawyers, and somewhat more numerical data from court administrators and judges. The system not sample public and consumer attitudes. Token "nonprofessionals" were appointed to some bar and Supreme Court committees and commissions. These were usually appointed because it was politically desirable to have them participate (i.e., selected members of the legislature).

The system will continually self-adjust, based on management's responses to information systems designed to assure dynamism and growth

The judiciary and the bar have never been fond of dynamism and growth. Wanting to keep things "as is" and opposing change have been hallmarks of the legal profession. Precedent is vital to them in more than deciding cases. Judges want to run the court system, and succeed in doing so. There is little in the training or experience of lawyers (and judges are simply lawyers in another role) that commends them to management roles. Florida's system, as that in other jurisdictions, lacked meaningful management systems, but was "growing" them under the guidance of Ken Palmer, Florida's capable state court administrator. The system was driven by many concerns, management information being only one of them.

The costs of the system will remain proportionate to its continuing benefits as benefits are perceived by consumers, public, providers and managers

Consumers and the public have not perceived any American court system as reasonably priced in years, perhaps not ever. Providers—lawyers and judges—for the most part thought things were costly, but worth it. When a population enjoys a monopoly (i.e., try to get a divorce in some other forum), competition between monopoly holders is the only pressure on pricing. Until antitrust considerations halted the practice in the seventies, many local Florida bar associations had "minimum fee schedules" that set the lowest price an "ethical" lawyer would charge for common services. Court managers had little information about the issue and little authority to deal with it. They stuck to counting cases and spotting lazy judges through their statistical microscopes.

So! That done, we'll turn to what was done to find a way to improve Florida's system. For a discussion framework, we will apply the Dispute Management order of work:

Present and possible future consumers of dispute resolution services will be identified

The Study Commission held a series of meetings for their education. The Commission brought authorities from around the nation to aid in the process. Next, it held public hearings in Florida's urban centers. The Commission learned how neighborhood dispute resolution centers were helping people who never had to resort to the courts. It learned that people, once ordered to go to mediation, returned to mediate later disputes without being told to go. Present consumers were easily identified. The future was more of the same, and included an interesting possibility. If access was simplified, would people not presently using the court system begin to turn to it? Could costs be reduced to enhance the use of the system by the near-poor? If so, the system could have more meaning in the lives of Florida's people. Commission members made recommendations to make mediation broadly available, but legislation for this change was not adopted. The model remained, "First you gotta sue 'em, then you can have court-ordered mediation."[4]

---

4.   This isn't a dead issue. Several State Justice Institute Commissions and Workshops are making recommendations to modify Florida's family courts along lines similar to those I recommended in 1972. Simple access to inexpensive dispute resolution may yet occur!

Demographic characteristics of populations of consumers will be related to the types of disputes of which they complain

The Florida Commission did not do this. It was beyond our scope, and outside our budget. Had we done so, we might have anticipated the emergence of an increasing number of people who wanted to handle their divorces,without any aid from lawyers. The 1988 system was not designed or equipped to handle these people.

Processes for dispute resolution, world wide, will be identified and catalogued

The Commission did not do this. It did consider mediation the most fundamental of dispute resolution mechanisms to use a third part. Mediation became the cornerstone of the new system. It also recommended use of non-binding ("advisory" in this book) arbitration and a form of voluntary binding arbitration that met the criticisms of traditional forms of binding, commercial arbitration.[5]

Processes responding to consumer needs and demographics will be chosen

Only in a coarse way did the Commission try to match consumer needs to processes. We recognized that the population of litigants forced to use the courts generally complained about the time, cost, and complexity of adversary processes. We knew that mediation had demonstrated its ability to answer these complaints. We knew, too, that some litigants would require that a third party make a decision for them. For them, we provided arbitration. The existing system of adversary trials was retained for cases in which the parties were willing to spend more time and money in order to gain the right to "discover" information from the adversary, to have a judge or jury decide the case, and a right to have an appeal.

---

5.   Court ordered and provided mediation of cases has proven so successful that the arbitration devices have been used fewer than one hundred times since 1988.

How much of the work can be done privately, how much must be performed by government?

We believed that most of the mediation work could be performed by private enterprise and need not be funded by tax revenues. Our public hearings had confirmed our personal belief that litigants would privately pay for earlier and more satisfying resolution of their cases. We were aware that the courts and bar would have to provide for mediation of indigents' cases.

The process array will be established

The legislation we proposed made both court-ordered mediation and non-binding arbitration available in all of Florida's courts. We made binding arbitration available for litigants who agreed the use of the process. The Commission's concepts left the existing mechanisms for civil adversary trials in place, unaltered. The array of formal processes had now been broadened to include voluntary mediation on agreement of the parties to a suit, court-ordered mediation, voluntary-binding arbitration with a limited appeal to the Circuit Court (Florida's general jurisdiction trial court), court-ordered non-binding arbitration, and adversary trials.

In the passage of the one bill, Florida had importantly altered the centuries old structure of the court system. Instead of offering only one process for dispute resolution, there were now five processes offered within the court system as formal functions of the judicial branch.

Rules for both substantive and procedural aspects will be drafted and adopted

Shortly after passage of the enabling bill, Florida's Supreme Court created a new committee to consider and recommend rules of civil procedure that would provide access to the several processes of the new system. I was asked to chair the Committee. Within four months, the Committee had completed its recommendations. We covered issues ranging from the qualifications and training of the mediators and arbitrators to who had to attend conferences. The Court unanimously approved the Committee's recommendations.[6]

Management information systems will be designed and tested to assure adequate and continuous feedback of efficiency and attitudinal data to system managers
Management methods will be implemented to assure continuous and immediate correction within the system, as near as possible to the points of service delivery
Communication will be planned for system wide access to information about performance, modifications and needs.

The Florida solution for these three items on the work list was to create and fund a Dispute Resolution Center. It was initially a function of Florida State University's College of Law and the Administrative Office of the Courts. The organization was ultimately transferred to the total control of the state Court Administrator The work on these three management concerns was attenuated by concerns of budget and time of available personnel. The Center gives continuing support to the Committees of the Supreme Court that is responsible for all aspects of the mediation and arbitration components of the new system. The Center maintains contact with organs of the Court that are responsible for contact with the adversary aspects of the system and special purpose groups, such as the one created to deal with the increasing number of

---

6. Rule 1.700, et. seq., Florida Rules of Civil Procedure, 1988. These rules have been extensively modified as we gained experience with the new court system. Most of the modifications are improvements, others seem little more than expressions of lawyers' love of making rules and their empty hope for controlling the universe with written statements! The only opposition to the adoption of the new rules came from the Trial Section of The Florida Bar. They opposed the provisions permitting judges to order lawyers and their parties to attend mediation in an effort to settle cases.

people who want to pursue their own divorces without the help of lawyers.

Staffing begins—Process managers will be chosen

The Dispute Resolution Center, managers at the local court level,
Administrative Judges and individual trial court judges in the Circuit
and County Court systems became the "managers" for implementation
of the process. The system was designed by the Commission and the
later rules Committee so that no new infrastructure or personnel would
be required to permit it to operate. Disputants would choose a process,
or judges would simply enter orders to cause one of the new processes
to be used. But government, being what it is, created beauracracies in
several of Florida's urban areas to provide and "regulate" the service.
Two of these agencies went so far as to provide billing and collection
services for the private mediators appointed to mediate cases[7].

Staffing begins-Service providers will be chosen

The work of deciding who would provide mediation and arbitration
services to the courts was begun by the Supreme Court's Mediation
and Arbitration Rules Committee. Since Judges were permitted to
order people to use mediators, a process was designed for "certification" of mediators. A judge was not permitted to order referral of a case
except to a certified mediator. We sought quality control through
requirements of high levels of education (all certified civil case mediators have a minimum of two college degrees) and experience in a field
related to the problems that they would be handling. We made distinctions between mediating family law cases, and other civil cases. We
specified that lawyers, CPA's, and people with advanced degrees in
mental health could be certified for family mediation.

  In a controversial move, the Committee recommended that only
lawyers should be permitted to become "certified" as civil case media-

---

7.   Hillsborough and Pinellas Counties (Tampa and St. Petersburg).

tors for cases other than family law matters. Nationally, this was perceived by many as an effort to end access to mediation work to non-lawyers. Certainly that was the effect.

The reason for the distinction came from concerns over lawyer acceptance of non-lawyer mediators. We knew that the major initial audience for the new system was the trial bar. Most of these lawyers opposed adoption of the system. They did not like the idea that a judge could force them to take their cases to mediation.

To become a permanent part of our court system, the new methods would have to be accepted by the trial bar. Within a few years the system was modified to permit any person to mediate any case, as long as the parties agreed and the person was qualified by training or experience to mediate cases. By then, lawyer acceptance of the system was complete, and the need for care could be relaxed.

Training begins
Process managers will be trained

Florida did not formally train its process managers. Everyone learned "on the job" or brought knowledge from previous exposure to the new processes.

Training begins
Service providers will be trained

The Rules of Civil Procedure for mediation and arbitration were adopted early in 1988. The Court Administrator contracted for mediation training for the mediators to be certified for use in the new system. My company, Dispute Management, Inc., organized a consortium of trainers. We designed a course and won the competition for the contract.

In April and May of 1988 we trained Florida's first Court Certified County Court, Family and Civil Mediators. They began work immediately.

Interestingly, the training has never stopped. Demand for mediation training has been continuous since 1988 and today forms a substantial part of the work of Dispute Management, Inc..[8]

Consumers will be informed about the system, and intake will begin

A big thank you to the media!

There were no funds for advertising the changes to the system. Media support for the changes had helped bring it about, and media attention provided consumers with knowledge of the system. More would have been better, as in programs for public schools, and speakers' programs, but funds were not available.

Feedback and response begin at the management level
Fine tuning begins—and never ends

This is the work of the Supreme Court, its Committees, and the Dispute Resolution Center. It has been effectively done, although funds have limited the level of information gathering and study that has gone on.

Public, consumer, provider and management satisfaction measurement begins—and never ends

Florida is not doing this satisfactorily. The public and the consumer are not included in the polling about the system. There is no formal means of measuring the levels of satisfaction of these important constituencies. Informal feedback to mediators and others providing services suggest that the changes are welcomed. We don't know how we might improve. If left to the lawyers and judges on the Committees, we'll see more and more new rules, as well as refinements of old ones. It's what we always do. The legal profession is too easily satisfied with

---

8.   Thousands of Florida's lawyers have taken mediation training. The response to the new system has been gratifying indeed.

abstractions and rules. We need more input from litigants and those who *don't* use the courts. Are they uninformed about the changes?

Fine tuning and modification is the continuous response of the system to management data it generates

If the system generated adequate information and was adequately funded, this would happen. So far, changes are generated at committee meetings as people argue for change, based on abstractions about dispute resolution or personal experience. Little actual data is gathered and not much processing of available data is going on.

It's time now to apply the principles to see if the work order led to the desired results.

The system will move adequate numbers of cases to resolution

It worked! Although case filings continue at a high rate, Florida's bar and public seem generally satisfied with what was done[9]. Most cases can be resolved in most of Florida's communities within months of filing, not years. Those that insist on trial will have a longer wait, but the removal of so many cases from court dockets by mediation alone has made the wait for trial much shorter. The numbers are impressive. With thousands of cases counted, Florida has proven that sixty-five per cent of all cases referred to mediation settle and are ended at the first mediation conference. We find a more impressive statistic in the percentage of cases going from filing to a final decision by a judge or jury.

Florida, like most states, historically found about five percent of the total of filed cases required a jury's verdict or a judge's decision. Since 1988 that percentage has dropped to one per cent! That is an eighty

---

9.   Only rough measurements are available. The fact that our legislature is not being asked to alter the system suggests and acceptable level of public approval. The Chair of the Mediation and Arbitration Rules Committee of the Florida Supreme Court believes no changes to the Rules of Civil Procedure are called for at this time. Scattered informal attitudinal surveys indicate that consumers are positive about their case mediation experiences.

per cent reduction in the time judges must put into trials and hearings. The reduction is reflected in the lowered need for additional judges in Florida, providing still more savings to the public.

The system will resolve cases quickly

Mediation conferences usually last only two to four hours! More complex cases require more time, of course. Most cases are not that complex. I mediated a case involving construction of a school in Indiana. The case had been pending for ten years. With the help at mediation, the parties to this case had settled it and had drafted a written settlement agreement by 6 PM the day of the mediation conference. I was on a plane home after just a day's work. Had I been a judge required to preside over the trial of this dispute, this case would have taken weeks of my life.

Cases are now being resolved even before they are filed and become "cases" for court management statistical purposes. Early settlements through mediation have become common for Florida litigants. Initially, settlements through mediation were occurring just before trial. That was not much help in clearing dockets. Since then, judges and lawyers have learned to attempt mediation much earlier, as the percentage of success is high.

The system will be simple enough that most people can use it without special assistance for the greatest possible numbers of cases

The arbitration and mediation processes satisfy this criterion. However, we have not succeeded in informing people of these processes, nor have we explained their use to potential consumers. Funds are needed to provide the public education required to encourage and permit public use. Another problem lies in the fact that the use of the system continues to require that a lawsuit be filed as an adversary proceeding before access to court ordered mediation can occur. I have suggested rule changes permitting people to simply and directly request court ordered mediation of their disputes. A user should not have to hire a lawyer to use such a simple process as mediation. Information and access need to be provided.

The system will emphasize redundancy of path, and variety of method for dispute resolution

Florida succeeded in this, but there is much more we can do. Direct filing for mediation, advisory opinions, inquisitorial trials, fast track, no-discovery trials, and court-regulated discovery without the necessity of first suing someone are a few of the paths and methods we could add. Some of these will come about with more ease than others. Presently, direct filing for mediation and fast-track trials seem to be realistic possibilities for the next few years. Am I being an optimist again?

The system will move each case to the most appropriate dispute resolution path—to the simplest method likely to be effective for the dispute and its owners

These decisions are presently being made by lawyers, and secondarily by clients of lawyers. Knowledgeable clients, such as E. I. du Pont de Nemours, are heavy users of mediated settlement conferences in Florida, but many litigants are unaware at how early settlement of their cases could be accomplished. Moving them from the expensive litigation path to the quicker, simpler, and faster mediation and arbitration tracks is a goal we continue to pursue. It is positive for the system that almost all Florida cases are mediated at some time in their course toward the courtroom. Now we must concentrate on getting them into an alternative process as early as possible.

The system will permit cases of possible social concern or precedential value to be identified and considered differently

We aren't doing this. If we had more paths and processes, it would be realistic to urge, but we can't succeed at this until we've solved the issue of redundancy.

The system will encourage and support the establishment of private dispute resolution—interpersonal, intra-organization and inter-organization

We succeeded here. There are many individuals and a few small companies that are providing dispute resolution services. The issue now is to encourage individuals to use these methods for their disputes, rather than using lawsuits. We'll have to provide more direct access before this can occur. I refer to the problem of having to file a lawsuit before you can get court-ordered mediation. Organizations are beginning to toy with, even implement the idea of internal dispute resolution systems for employee disputes. The seed has been planted.

The system will move cases that can be handled privately into private dispute resolution and out of government channels

Another success. Most civil cases in Florida are mediated by independent contractors, trained and certified through the system conceived by the Committee.

The system will, wherever feasible and to the extent possible, collect its cost from users

Litigants pay for mediation. Litigants pay for the service, even if ordered to mediation by the court. If not mediated privately, family law cases are most likely to be mediated by a government employee in urban areas of the state. Provision for mediation for the indigent is made through local bar associations' legal aid committees. For example, if I am told that one of the litigants in a case is being represented by a volunteer legal aid lawyer, I will provide mediation free-of-charge.

The system will gain feed back from consumers, the public, its providers, and its managers
The system will continually self adjust, based on

management's responses to information systems designed to assure dynamism and growth

Because of limited funds, the Florida system only partially succeeds at meeting these criteria. The rough mechanisms are in place through the office of the State Court Administrator and the Dispute Resolution Center. Without funding, measurement is beyond reach for these agencies. If we could measure consumer and public attitudes and needs, we could further refine our system in a rational way.

The costs of the system will remain proportionate to its continuing benefits as benefits are perceived by consumers, public, providers and managers

The changes to the system have not been costly. The benefits obtained have been great, as perceived by the managers and providers. Limited private polling of litigants who have had their cases exposed to mediation, whether they were resolved or not, has revealed high levels of satisfaction, both with the certified mediators and with the process.

An incidental observation is in order about an anomaly.

Our Commission thought that lawyers would use the arbitration devices we drafted into the proposed legislation. They have not. Our assumption was based on the undying loyalty of trial lawyers to adversary trial processes. We thought we were offering a simpler, cheaper adversary process that would find favor with business litigants in particular. We labored to craft the processes to avoid the common criticisms voiced by lawyers and other users about classic "binding" arbitration.

Florida's trial bar fell in love with mediation. They learned that they did not lose control of outcomes in mediation as they do in arbitrations and trials. They learned that their clients were pleased with the mediation process and could play a larger role in it than in the trial.

In sum, arbitration has been ignored. As an abstraction, it is a good idea. In reality, it seems to meet no current need. Could public education about the processes cause them to be chosen more often? Without measurement and feedback about public and consumer attitudes, we cannot know.

Finally, a personal confession. Throughout the years of my work on this project, I never talked of or published my thinking about the Dispute Management concept. I was concerned that the audience of judges and attorneys I needed to convince would believe these ideas too revolutionary. If so, they would not be applied.

I first spoke of a few of the principles when presenting the report of the Rules Committee in a formal hearing before the Supreme Court of Florida early in 1988. One of the Committee members accused me of inventing them on the spot! I told the Court we had been guided by those principles. I never told them that I *told* the Committee members that we were being guided by them.

7

A Model Court System: Justice á la Carte

We have taken inventory of dispute resolution processes. We next studied application of Dispute Management principles to a State Court system. In this Chapter we'll see what could result, and how much more useful it would be to consumers of dispute resolution services.

The following pages describe a marvelously rich, redundant dispute resolution system. Lawyers may recoil, as "redundant" is an objectionable concept in their jargon. Lawyers are often folks who see the work as a set of binary propositions—something is, or it is not. The perception that there could be many paths toward dispute resolution may not be comfortable for some of our legal-trained neighbors.

Redundancies of paths to outcomes and redundancy of process create new opportunities for personal, corporate, and government Dispute Management. Within a redundant system, permutations and combinations of process become possible. With our present adversarial system there is but one process, and combination and permutation is not possible.

For people seeking freedom of choice, the a′ la carte courthouse is a good destination. Just what processes could be assembled for delivery at the courthouse, and how might the system work?

The operational principle behind the success of Florida-like systems is the addition of varying *processes* for dispute resolution, not a redefinition of *remedies* available through litigation or new *rules* of procedure, evidence, or *causes of action*.

Recall as well that we are in the process of *adding* processes, not eliminating litigation and the adversary process it employs. The institution of the public trial is far too important in our democratic republic to brook conversation about its elimination. We added mediation and arbitration as parallel processes, not substitutes.

In the late seventies, Professor and Dean Frank E. A. Sander of Harvard broke new and important ground with his Pound Lecture, describing a "multi-door courthouse." Prof. Sander pointed out that there were indeed multiple processes and many community-based resources for dispute resolution. His concern was to provide a means of access to these processes and resources.

In the "multidoor courthouse" concept, we find a means of adding to the resolution processes available to disputants, but many of us lose interest when we learn that "the key feature of the multidoor courthouse is the initial procedure: intake screening. Here disputes would be analyzed according to various criteria to determine what mechanism would be best suited for the resolution of the problem" and that "…a sophisticated intake officer would analyze the dispute and refer it (to the process) most likely to resolve it effectively[1]."

Why not let litigants choose processes when filing? Many of us are worn thin with the decisions others try to make "for our own good." We prefer freedom of choice over the choices of even a "sophisticated intake officer," perhaps especially over such a person's choices!

Disagreements about choice of process can be resolved by judges or hearing officers. Freedom of choice can be granted to litigants. Bar and bench are learning of new processes and will be competent to make acceptable decisions about process. Why increase the size and cost of conflict resolution with unnecessary officials?

Processes can be provided *within* the judicial system and through the bar to eliminate the need for "alternative" dispute resolution. That phrase was invented by people who rejected the traditional role of the bench and bar in dispute resolution in favor of "alternatives." We

---

1.   Dispute Resolution, Goldberg, Green and Sander, 1985, pp 415-416

should seek more dispute resolution from the judicial branch, not dilution of its function. Dispute resolution is a major organic and constitutional justification for the judicial branch.

What can we do to transform America's courts from simplistic adversary litigation providers into a dispute resolution *system*? Here is a menu of processes that might work together:

Full-discovery, "traditional" adversarial trial processes

A judicial "forecast"

Court-mandated and supervised mediation in full-discovery cases

Fast-track, "simplified" scant-discovery trial processes

Privately employed public judges

Stipulated mediation in fast-track cases

Direct filing for mandated mediation without having to first file a lawsuit.

Supervised Discovery without having to first file a lawsuit

Advisory arbitration

Non-binding arbitration

Court supervised binding arbitration

Inquiry Courts

Combined processes using two or more of the listed ideas

Advisory judicial panels

FULL DISCOVERY, ADVERSARY TRIALS

We would continue to offer adversary trials with full discovery. Contemporary litigation processes are highly evolved. They are utilitarian for dealing with cases in which necessary information is likely to be withheld. Adversary discovery is useful for gathering a quantity of information to be placed, ultimately, before appellate courts.

The full-bore adversary system is overkill for the problems encountered due to a rear-end collision at an intersection, with predictable lesions of the cervical spine. Such cases—and such simple cases are the great majority of cases filed—involve no social issues, or complex factual problems, or policy issues of governmental, business or personal importance. They are readily understood and long-standing principles and practices of law are available for their resolution.

So what might we offer in addition to full-bore adversary litigation as enhancements for the system? What process would be better for the simpler, more ordinary fare of local courts?

JUDICIAL FORECASTS

Today, some judges invite counsel to tell them about their cases, often at a pre-trial conference. These judges then put the "writing on the wall," forecasting the outcome of the case, assuming certain truths about how evidence will be received, and how the judge will react to the law.

This practice has truly ancient precedents, although it seems at odds with the way lawyers and judges have perceived the role of the judiciary in this century. The Anglo-Saxon "judges" "...reached a winner-take-all legal judgment and announced it to the parties, but before those judgments were finalized by oath-swearing the third-party decision makers often persuaded the losing party to come to terms with the winning party, fostering their reconciliation."[2]

Judges, or other judicial personnel, could in one or more conferences with counsel, begin the evaluation of the law as it applies to a case from its earliest stages. If parties can know how the court believes the law would apply to evidentiary, procedural and substantive issues, the likelihood of settlement will increase as an understanding of probable outcomes emerges. This will enhance the parties' ability to more

2.   Sanchez, Valerie A., Towards a History of ADR: The Dispute Processing Continuum in Anglo-Saxon England and Today, The Ohio State Journal On Dispute Resolution, v.11, No. 1, 1996

accurately estimate probabilities, quantify and value possible outcomes, then appraise settlement approaches. Common perceptions of appropriate settlements become more likely as well. As a mediator, I recognize this environment as one in which settlement is most likely.

FAST TRACK, SIMPLIFIED LITIGATION

What about "shoot-out" trials?

Until this century, there was virtually no discovery, unless voluntarily provided. Lawyers might exchange some information. While blasting away with the obvious, they often kept a strategic or tactical derringer in a boot.

Trial was far more dramatic then than now. What lawyers said and did in courtrooms mattered far more than what today's trudging mavens of discovery eventually disgorge in courtrooms. Whereas adversary trial in a discovery system is more of a yawning anti-climax, trial in a limited discovery system was pure excitement. It was why people crowded the squares of county seats on trial days.

In the shoot-out trial process, one would file a suit observing the conventions of contemporary litigation about parties, causes of action, and remedies. In addition, a demand for this form of adversary trial will be added. Perhaps somewhere in the claim for relief we would find a line stating that in addition to a jury trial, this litigant wanted a shoot out. If forced to be more dignified, perhaps the pleader would ask for "simplified" or "fast track" litigation.

That phrase would then stimulate the defending party to either accept the simpler trial or to move the court for full-bore, discovery-driven litigation. Judges would be told to presume that the fast-track is the best process when parties do not agree on process.

Within a prescribed time following service of process, a simultaneous exchange of all tangible items that might be used in evidence, together with sworn summaries of testimony, would be exchanged by counsel. Total failure to exchange by the plaintiff would result in dismissal. Total failure to exchange by the defendant would result in an immediate default, permitting the plaintiff to seek immediate judgment.

The trial date would be set at the time of filing the case. Cases would be docketed before divisions of the court designated for handling simplified trials. Continuance would occur only because of a backlog. Legislatures would take responsibility for adequate judicial organization and staffing to prevent backlog. It may be necessary to add judges to these divisions, as more Americans find they can again afford lawyers, and access to their courts.

At trial, the guiding rule for the bench would be to permit only evidence that was exchanged or could be readily inferred from that exchanged. Nothing further would be admitted, even though in compliance with existing evidence codes.

These trials would be scheduled for a brief period of time. Perhaps three days would be the maximum permitted. Each side would be entitled to use precisely half the time, as they saw fit. The judge would act as referee and timekeeper. No extensions to the time would be permitted. At the end of the third day the case would be submitted to the judge or jury.

PRIVATELY-EMPLOYED PUBLIC JUDGES

These are judges for one case only. They will have all the powers and responsibilities of elected or appointed judges, but only as to the case for which counsel has selected them. The trials they conduct will be public trials with public records. Appeals can be taken as from the rulings of full-time judges. Jurisdiction is as broad as that of other judges on the same bench. They are compensated entirely by the parties. California offers a model for such an addition to the new judicial branch.

Arbitration would be attractive in many divorce proceedings, but too many issues—such as the welfare of children—prohibit the use of the process. A privately employed judge could be granted authority to make these decisions, as they would be subject to the usual appellate processes.

Another objection to binding arbitration stems from the lack of meaningful review or appeal. Appeals would be available from private judges, as from public ones.

Privately employed judges bring other advantages. Consider fixed trial dates, agreed hours and days for trials, and as much flexibility in managing the events of trial as counsel wish. Add to this a tolerant, interested judge, known to be competent in the substantive area involved and this option takes on new meaning.

COURT-MANDATED MEDIATION

In our system, we now see litigation with discovery joined by a second process: the simplified trial. This change is not enough. It only meets two of the public objections to our work: that it is too slow and that it is too expensive.

We must meet the final objection: that the judicial branch is too complicated to use. Not everyone needs an *adversary* process or the formality of trial to resolve a dispute. Other processes must be considered as additions to the expanded judicial branch.

In Florida we have learned that between 95 and 98 percent of all litigation filed is disposed of without a jury verdict or a judge's decision. Thousands of these cases are being disposed of through formal, court-mandated mediation conducted after filing a conventional lawsuit. We hear also that cases are being disposed of by mediation before litigation has commenced.

Mediation is a simple process. It is unencumbered by limitations of remedy, cause of action, parties, rules of procedure, and evidence. It has no formal internal process and is essentially negotiation-guided, enhanced, and assisted by a mediator.

Judges in full-discovery cases would be permitted to order mediation. They would be limited to requiring use of mediators trained for the work who meet both academic and experience requirements provided by statute or rule. Florida's system of court-mandated mediation provides a working, successful model of a litigant-financed process.

Judges would not be permitted to mandate mediation in fast-track cases. The parties would be permitted to stipulate to mediation of these cases.

DIRECT FILING FOR MEDIATION

Why should our new system insist on filing a lawsuit before permitting mediation?

At present we sometimes file suit to force passive adversaries to the bargaining table. In systems that provide it, we then seek mandated mediation at first opportunity in an effort to speedily resolve a client's case. Why be indirect? We should add mandated mediation, on demand, to the menu.

A petition would be filed resulting in the issuance of a summons to the adversary, requiring attendance at a mediation session at a preset time and place. The issues for mediation would be stated in the petition. The petition would include an offer to exchange information helpful to negotiations and would request specified information. Compliance would be voluntary, but unless exchanged, existing information could not be admitted in evidence in a later adversary process.

The mediator would be trained and certified by the court system. If the parties disagreed with the court's choice of mediator, a mutually agreed mediator would be used. The filing party would pay the mediator.

If the mediation did not result in disposition of the case through settlement, then either party would have the option of to proceed to the full-discovery or simplified litigation tracks. There would be no further mediation ordered by the courts unless upon stipulation of the parties or upon grant of a motion by either party for further mediation.

SUPERVISED DISCOVERY WITHOUT HAVING TO FIRST FILE A LAWSUIT

A lawsuit may produce a malpractice claim or a claim of malicious prosecution, or both. Abuse of process is a rare but threatening possibility.

There are times when lack of information may provoke a suit. If the suit proves improvident after discovery, it can provoke the counterattack. More time burnt from the limited supply of American courts! Why not permit an uncertain, exploring litigant to move for specified discovery, subject to supervision by a court-appointed official?

The immediate objection is that such a process might be used to harass, to economically injure a weaker adversary in bargaining, or in competition. Well, lawsuits are used this way, without any means of regulation. A party intent on pursuing an ulterior goal will do so with lawsuits. Erstwhile litigants, if proceeding in good faith from a position of ignorance, will choose regulated discovery.

Will it be used to learn trade secrets or to gain unique competitive advantages?

No doubt people will try. That is why one of the court's trained arbitrators will be appointed to supervise, to be immediately available to resolve disputes over what may be asked and what may be seen. The court's initial ruling on the motion for supervised discovery will outline the permitted scope of inquiry. The rule of procedure implementing the process will instruct the supervisor to bias all decisions in favor of privacy, not disclosure, contrary to the bias in full-discovery litigation cases.

A party may well voluntarily disclose, rather than face the alternative of forcing the adversary toward full-discovery litigation with its attendant expense and risk.

This process may well pressure a party toward mediation and settlement of a claim. That is what usually happens after full-discovery litigation. We should expect to see the same here, but without another case to crowd yet another docket.

ADVISORY ARBITRATION

Advisory arbitration results in an award, but one that is not binding. No party is penalized or exposed to additional costs for refusing to be bound by an award. Advisory arbitration would be used by judges through mandate, or voluntarily by the parties, when a significant legal issue bars settlement.

Perceptions of cases are driven by perceptions of "the law." When those perceptions are at odds, settlement cannot occur. The values driven by relative perceptions are too often so grossly different that it is impossible to find common ground.

However, the advice of peer arbitrators will provide an assessment of the likelihood of a precedent being established. This process could be confidential as well, so as not to risk influencing the outcome in court should advisory arbitration fail to result in settlement.

NON-BINDING ARBITRATION

Non-binding arbitration has been tried in a number of federal jurisdictions and in several state courts. It is binding if the award of the attorney-arbitrators is accepted. If not accepted, the accepting party's costs from the date of tendered acceptance might be assessed against the non-accepting party, should the non-accepting party fail at trial to obtain a result as favorable as the arbitration award.

Under non-binding arbitration schemes, arbitration is court-mandated, or may be chosen by the parties. An attenuated hearing is held, at which summary evidence and arguments are presented to a panel of usually three attorney-arbitrators. The attorney-arbitrators return their award after a brief deliberation.

The award is final, unless a party opts for a trial "de novo." When a party opts for a trial, the party is making a wager that the outcome of the trial will be better than that of the arbitration, thereby escaping a possible court order to pay the opponent's attorney fees and costs.

BINDING ARBITRATION

Florida makes two forms of binding arbitration available. One is statutory, along the lines of the Uniform Arbitration Law. The other is made available as a *court* process.

Rules of civil procedure permit a court file to be maintained as for litigation and allow review of the award by a trial court judge. This arbitration is "fast-track," with the intention that disputes might be rapidly ended with the assistance of trained attorney-arbitrators. Although designed for commercial and business issues, it is not limited in use.

Mediation and arbitration might not be restricted by classical legal definitions of remedy. Anything lawful, in principle, can be a "remedy" in mediation and arbitration. Judicial discretion standards would not apply to arbitration, and therefore some areas of inquiry (i.e., the custody and support of children) might be excluded from the process.

CIVIL INQUIRY COURTS

Inquiry courts use judges differently. In this process, the judge is an active, guiding, and powerful decision-maker. Adversarial trial judges are expected to remain passive during trials. The inquisitorial judge is part investigator, part decision-maker.

An inquisitorial process would be most useful in cases involving difficult concepts of technology, science, or economics. Use of the process would be an option for parties in these cases.

The process would also be apt for dealing with interpersonal relationship issues, as in dissolving marriages. The increased "gripping power" of the inquisitorial judge will permit the court to deter these cases from runaway discovery and from becoming motion-monsters. A less-empowered, passive adversary process judge cannot adequately control these cases. Use of the inquisitorial process might be required for relationship cases, such as dissolution of marriages.

A Civil Inquiry Court could have an additional discretionary jurisdiction. Sometimes lawsuits are filed out of ignorance or an inability to acquire critical information. Such "suspicion" suits would be filed in Civil Inquiry Court, alleging the need for specified discovery. The defendant could provide the information or contest the pleader's right to have it (as in the case of secret, or proprietary information). The court would determine whether it should preside over the limited discovery process, what conditions should be imposed (e.g., secrecy), or perhaps refer its management to a master to be compensated by the pleader. Once completed, the matter would either be dismissed or transformed to one of the other forms of dispute resolution available in the system.

COMBINING PROCESSES FOR SPECIAL TYPES OF CASES

What about handling family problems? There is substantial evidence that most family matters are best handled in mediation. Most of these cases will resolve themselves, with the help of a trained mediator. Why not permit parties to choose simpler methods for resolving divorce and dissolution issues?

Part of the process of simplification will be to provide combined, sequential use of mediation and an inquiry court. The presiding judge will actively manage cases from filing to judgment and take a role in deciding the issues to be pursued and in securing production of needed evidence. Initial work with the parties will be by the mediator in an effort to permit settlement of as many cases as possible in a non-adversarial environment. If any issue remains unresolved, the inquisitorial court will become active. The judge works with the parties and counsel to determine what information is needed. Next it will secure and evaluate that information. Finally, after taking designated testimony and hearing final arguments, the court will decide the outstanding issues.

Mediation will be the new system's first response to parties seeking termination of a marriage, resolution of issues concerning children, paternity, and perhaps "juvenile law" issues. Critical early case issues—such as hot and unresolved disputes over children's residence—would be referred to the presiding judge for an initial, probationary decision. Of course when parties agree, the mediator would provide a draft agreement and order to the judge for entry.

The judge will "preside" over the divorce process as a process manager and will be empowered to require the parties to produce information requested by the mediator, and not voluntarily provided. The judge and mediator will work as a team to first assist the parties in finding their own resolutions, then to provide adjudication of remaining issues.

For the small percentage of these cases requiring an adversary hearing, the inquisitorial process will be appropriate. Rules of evidence would be relaxed to a simple rule, permitting the presiding judge to decide what would be relevant to the decision to be made. The judge could require production of such information. Trials would likely be a series of brief hearings, conducted until the judge was satisfied with the information available, then a decision would be made.

Such a combined process will aid the increasing numbers of pro se litigants in family cases.

ADVISORY JUDICIAL PANELS

It would save us time and money if we could get advice from our judges about the possible outcomes of potential lawsuits. If we could, we would see the system as more responsive, less time consuming, and less expensive. We might also think it less complicated if we could simply go to Solomon with our problems.

We cannot get advice from our judges. Why not? Because we think advisory opinions could embarrass the courts if, in a later full-discovery proceeding the ruling were to change.

We need advice from our judges. They could help forestall more serious disputes, perhaps even public violence.

We could create a system in which parties could pursue full-discovery, advisory opinions, or fast-track limited discovery advisory opinions.

Panels of judges could be formally approached by governments and organizations for the purpose of obtaining advisory opinions on issues described in their petitions.

Judges would be permitted to decline to convene a panel or to act as a panelist. Judges would be encouraged to participate when social issues affecting cognizable groups were involved.

These rulings would be in no way binding and could be later reversed, modified, or abandoned by any and all of the judges on the panel.

The purpose is to provide informal, voluntary forums where people—with or without lawyers—could present issues and their views. The panelists would identify the groups and individuals appropriate to the discussions.

The judges would engage in dialogue with participants, ask for information, suggest lines of inquiry, query the contestants, debate the prospect of any given outcome, and would ultimately cast their ballots for an outcome. In truly puzzling cases it would be reasonable to expect—of the panel of three judges—three different views.

How would this be useful? It would be useful because of the reasoning process in which the public will see judges engage, and because of the public participation permitted by this process.

It may be that people would go on to resolve their disputes, even in the face of conflicting opinions by the judges. They would do so because of the demonstrated uncertainty of any given outcome of their dispute.

Obviously, where all of the judges agree, the dispute is more likely to be resolved. It is also possible that the affected parties will pursue appropriate legislative or constitutional change rather than approach the courts with the issue.

We can begin to provide the many paths of the a la carte courthouse as soon as we choose. There is, once more, no constitutional prohibition against it, and it will probably reduce the cost of government, not increase it.

8

Divorce—Let's Manage It!

It is too easy to marry, and so hard to divorce.

The emotional pain of a disappointing ending is bad enough. The sadness, embarrassment, and grieving that accompany the end of a once loving relationship are burdens of the first magnitude.

To add to our troubles, the only way out of a marriage is through the courthouse. To end our marriages, we have no alternative but to use the existing adversarial trial and litigation process. We have to *sue* each other, for goodness sake!

Remember, to be married, all you had to do was get a license and pay the preacher. You set the day, said the vows, celebrated with friends and were off to a rosy future.

To end your marriage you must hire a lawyer or try to find your way through the courthouse maze on your own. In lawyer talk, you become a "pro se" (sounds like "pro say") litigant.

If you want to blame someone for the current messy way of ending marriages, start with Henry VIII. The Roman Catholic Church wouldn't let him have the divorce and remarriage he wanted. Henry, resourceful King that he was, organized a new church and got what he wanted. He also began the English idea that the *State* should be involved with regulating marriage—and therefore divorce.

As centuries passed, getting married and un-married became the business of the government. It issued licenses to marry, kept the records that legitimized children, and assured passage of title to property. When time to divorce the government said, "Go see the judge." That was a mistake.

Some of us think divorce is sinful. These people want the rest of us to go to a judge for permission not to be married. They therefore wanted to make it impossible to do (these folks did relent slightly by permitting divorce upon proof of adultery), or at least very difficult to do.

Even in states making so-called "no-fault" divorce available, you will probably have to tell the judge something bad about your marriage to obtain the judge's blessing of your divorce.

We tout our belief in separation of church and state, and yet state laws reflect the attitudes of organized religious groups about divorce. To succeed at altering the divorce business to better meet our needs and realities, we will have to spar with both divorce lawyers and with fundamentalist, doctrinaire religious groups.

There are three aspects of ending a marriage that will require our consideration:

1. Ending the legal marriage—changing the legal relationship between the spouses and making them eligible for marriage to others;

2. Sorting out the property, income, liabilities and support needs of the spouses, and

3. Most importantly, providing for the psychological and financial needs of any children of the marriage.

If you need any further encouragement to consider changing the present system, take a moment to consider how we now handle divorce—with the attendant expense, complexity and delay. To do this, turn each one of the goals listed below into a question asked about the present system. You will quickly see how seriously it fails us.

How would the present system by altered if we apply the Dispute Management principles? It would be radically altered, and marvelously improved.

First, we list the Dispute Management system goals. They are:

The system will move adequate numbers of cases to resolution

The system will resolve cases quickly

The system will be simple enough that most people can use it without special assistance for the greatest possible numbers of cases

The system will emphasize redundancy of path and variety of method for dispute resolution

The system will move each case to the most appropriate dispute resolution path—to the simplest method likely to be effective for the dispute and its owners

The system will permit cases of possible social concern, or precedential value to be identified and considered differently

The system will encourage and support the establishment of private dispute resolution—interpersonal, intra-organization and inter-organization

The system will move cases that can be handled privately into private dispute resolution and out of government channels

The system will, wherever feasible and to the extent possible, collect its cost from users

The system will gain feedback from consumers, the public, its providers and its managers

The system will continually self-adjust, based on management's responses to information systems designed to assure dynamism and growth

The costs of the system will remain proportionate to its continuing benefits as benefits are perceived by consumers, public, providers and managers

Next, let's postulate a simple system and see if it satisfies our goals.

What if you got a divorce by going to the government and just telling it you were divorced and needed to register the fact? You would buy a license for divorce, just as you bought a license to marry.

To deal with our more mercurial neighbors, the license would be issued only after a thirty-day waiting period and a second trip to the courthouse to pay for the license and pick it up. Your spouse would be notified that you had applied for the license (just in case you were too shy to tell 'em) and would be told about spouse's rights in a general sense.

During the waiting period, both spouses would be required to attend a meeting with a trained mediator. This person would be educated in the laws that apply to divorces in your state. They would be permitted to give you information about how the laws worked and what might happen if you were to ask for a hearing before a hearing officer. They might or might not be lawyers. This person's job is to learn more about your family, and what disputes there might be between you and your spouse that need resolution. Their job is to help you and your spouse understand what is needed, how the system works, and what to expect from the process.

For this phase you could hire a private mediator, approved by the government for this work. Or, you could use the free mediator provided by the government.

The mediator would initiate inquiry into the needs of your children. The mediator might personally meet with your older kids, or if you and your spouse can't agree on where the younger ones should live, kick the inquiry to a family counselor. You'd be permitted to hire your own licensed counselor if you preferred and if you could afford to do so.

If there were conflicts and disputes, the mediator could not help you resolve within say sixty days, you would be referred to a special hearing officer for an inquisitorial hearing. Not inquisitional, but *inquisitorial!* The officer would help you both understand as much of the law as you needed to know and would make a decision about your disputes if you could not. The officer, as an inquisitorial judge, could investigate as required and conduct sessions on multiple days if needed. We would set a time limit on how long this process would be allowed to go on.

The hearing officer could be a public employee (provided without additional charge) or a person the spouses employ to provide the service privately. The decision of a licensed, privately-employed hearing officer would become a public record and would be just as binding as the decisions of hearing officers provided by government.

The penalty for failing to cooperate to make the process work would be an adverse decision by the hearing officer. This way, delay would not work to the advantage of a spouse choosing to be passive or to attempt delay by not cooperating in attending or providing information requested by the other spouse, the mediator, or ultimately the hearing officer.

Note that the divorce became final at the end of the thirty days after you applied. What has been going on since is the business of sorting out concerns over children and economics.

If you don't like the officer's decision, you can ask for review by a local judge. The judge would be allowed to turn you down, unless the officer had violated a guideline, a state law, or the constitution.

The mediator, the hearing officer and the judge would be encouraged to identify cases involving unique legal or social concerns for special handling (for example, when spouse abuse is alleged). Extended periods of time could be permitted for management of these cases. If the jurisdiction has an "a la carte" courthouse (See Chapter 8), then special processes might be designed to help spouses in unique cases.

Now, let's see if the goals of Dispute Management have been achieved.

The system will move adequate numbers of cases to resolution
The system will resolve cases quickly

Our simple and accessible system means that more cases can be handled by fewer public employees at lower compensation than judges. Our system will let spouses who have reached an agreement about their divorce complete the entire task in thirty days.

The system will be simple enough that most people can use it without special assistance, for the greatest possible numbers of cases

Spouses will not need lawyers to end marriages. The system is simple, and there will be a required stop at the desk of a knowledgeable and helpful mediator. Even today, almost all cases are ended in negotiated settlements. Our system makes it less expensive to obtain the same result, as we will no longer be dependent upon lawyers to guide us through the process. The providers (the mediator, and if required the hearing officer) will give us the information and the advice we need to make use of the system. We will be free to use a lawyer when we choose.

Judges and courtrooms should rarely see or hear of a family law case in our new system. There is no reason why the courts should continue to handle the great majority of family related cases. Judges will be necessary in those very, very few cases in which an issue of precedential importance occurs (remember, the courts are a source of "law" just as the legislature is the principal source of law). An administrative hearing officer will provide a forum for the pathological fighters and their unfortunate spouses. No robe, lower cost. No robe, greater access. No robe, different role. More of this later.

Mediation is a simple, natural, human and ancient way of working things out when one-on-one negotiation is not enough. Mediation should be the first response of the state in assuring that its interests in dissolving marriages are met.

In the new system, a person seeking a divorce ("dissolution of marriage" in some states) would go to the appropriate government office, purchase a license for dissolution, and would be provided information which would permit them to choose a private mediator or accept an appointment with a government employed mediator.

The license would become final and the divorce effective after uneventful passage of perhaps thirty days, or when the parties reach an agreement, or the hearing officer's rulings become final, assuring the support of the less wealthy spouse and the children. Finality will be evidenced by the endorsement and filing of the original license by the mediator or the hearing officer. The remaining property and support issues would be mediated or decided by the hearing officer in subsequent weeks.

The mediator's first task will be to understand the couple's relative stages in the grieving process (denial, anger, resignation, acceptance) and to start them on the path of gathering information necessary to an orderly and informed process.

Mediators should be permitted to legally advise both spouses. This idea will cause many lawyer readers discomfort. The bench and bar often think in binaries, and this is one of the issues to which such perceptions are applied. To legally trained people there are only two roles in applying law: judge or lawyer. Therefore, there are only two codes of ethical conduct: one for judges and a very different one for lawyers.

Both codes are built on the assumption that the adversary process is the only process in which they will engage. The thought of one lawyer advising two clients is anathema to lawyers and judges. The adversary system requires that a lawyer represent but one client and be that client's "zealous advocate." Recent televised trials have shown what kind of conduct that standard produces.

Our system will require a third standard: one for the lawyers and other professionals who mediate. To be of full service to the consuming public, the mediators trained for the system must be free to advise both spouses about courses of conduct open to them. This advice, and its negative and positive effects relative to the spouses, must be shared with both spouses. Each spouse will make the decision about what to do, as mediators are not judges and don't decide things for the people they serve.

Lawyers will tell you this just isn't possible, but they are trapped by their perceptions and unaware of the changes to the lawyer's role which have occurred in the last half of the twentieth century.

A few states have codes of conduct that reflect the "old way" (e.g., Indiana). Lawyers once counseled with both sides of a conflict in an effort to resolve it short of court. In smaller communities and in a slower time in America's history, lawyers served to help all their clients, neighbors and friends to end their disputes. *Lawyers mediated.*

It is necessary to revive this honored role for our lawyers. They will have to amend their standards of conduct to realize these values for our system.

Because of their concerns over liability to their clients, it will be reasonable to grant them immunity from their suits while they mediate. Florida has done so by statute, and other states have done so as appellate courts ruled on suits against lawyer mediators.[1] In exchange for immunity, they should be required to accept training as a mediator and should be required to adhere to the set of standards of conduct devised for mediators as they mediate. If they violate those standards, punishment could range from reprimands to disbarment.

The system will have to provide training to persons other than lawyers who wish to mediate for couples dissolving their marriages. There are extensive and complicated propositions of federal and state taxation, property law and local legislation concerning marriage and divorce, which should be understood. In the new system, we don't want neutrals to be forced to advise people in search of an answer, "Go

---

1.   Michigan, The District of Columbia, Maryland, and California to date.

find a lawyer because I am not allowed to talk with you about what you should know or what you should do!"

As much as a year of special, post-graduate education could be required. This could be offered as a masters' level curriculum at state universities having a law faculty available or at the local level[2].

We should decide to educate the lawyer mediators in the social sciences while we are at it. Their law degrees give absolutely no assurance that their understanding of child development, the psycho-dynamics of marriage and its dissolution, or the various therapeutic methods of conflict management will be sufficient to satisfy our high standards for handling these painful disruptions. Local resources for this training and education will again prove adequate.

It will be complicated and challenging to become one of the people who directly serve the public in our system, in exchange for making it simple and straightforward for the public to use the system.

The system will emphasize redundancy of path, and variety of method for dispute resolution
The system will move each case to the most appropriate dispute resolution path—to the simplest method likely to be effective for the dispute and its owners

Counseling, mediation, inquisitorial hearing and the many processes available in the a la carte courthouse will be used or will be available in our system. There are many paths, and there are people along the path to give us directions: the mediators and hearing officers. We are assured that the simplest method acceptable to us will always be made available to us.

---

2. Adjunct faculty, drawn from the local bar and bench is more than adequate for this task. Extension services as well as Junior and Community Colleges can provide these courses as full time, or night curricula

The system will permit cases of possible social concern, or precedential value to be identified and considered differently

The mediator and the hearing officer are empowered to encourage the judge to give special treatment to a case. A spouse can make the request directly to the judge, should the mediator and hearing officer disagree with the spouse about the need for a special process for the case. Few cases have precedential value, in the sense of the development of a coherent body of public law, but the system must have a way of recognizing when such a condition exists. At present, lawyers raise these issues in public trials, but the issue can be raised without the trial and need not be raised only by lawyers.

The system will encourage and support the establishment of private dispute resolution—interpersonal, intra-organization and inter-organization
The system will move cases that can be handled privately into private dispute resolution, and out of government channels

In this system a spouse can do everything required to legally end a marriage in privacy. Only in unique cases would a judge ever be required, and then only after the judge has decided the case is one over which s/he should exercise jurisdiction. No one could take a spouse to court just for vengeance.

Mediators and hearing officers can be trained and "certified" as mediators today in States like Florida, Indiana and North Carolina.

The system will, wherever feasible and to the extent possible, collect its cost from users

As long as our way of handling marriage and divorce is to pay more attention to divorce than to marriage, greater cost will be incurred by the public in dissolving marriages. We can fund this cost with higher fees for marriage licenses or by penalizing unsuccessful marriages with high fees for the divorce license.

The latter solution is poor. Divorce is a time when family finances are stretched to their limits. A more humane solution to the problem of funding and to meeting our goal of "users pay" is to collect the money government needs for divorce services, up front, at the time of issuing the marriage license. Some will argue that this will discourage marriage. Well, if it does, there will be less divorce, won't there?

The system will gain feedback from consumers, the public, its providers and its managers
The system will continually self-adjust, based on management's responses to information systems designed to assure dynamism and growth
The costs of the system will remain proportionate to its continuing benefits as benefits are perceived by consumers, public, providers and managers

These goals will be met as planned in Chapter 6, "Using Dispute Management Principles to Improve a State Court System." There will not be significant additional cost, as personnel hired to run our better courthouse will manage the lessened role of the courts in divorce, along with other duties.

There is no constitutional or practical reason for divorce to be the business of lawyers alone or for it to be so very difficult to accomplish. If we want to change, we can do so with simple legislation.

Passing the laws will be difficult, as the divorce lawyers and certain religious groups will oppose these laws strenuously.

9

Dispute Management for the Criminal Courts Creating a Third Path

We should first examine some of the most basic tenets of the American criminal justice system. The system makes the following assumptions, upon which all procedural and substantive legal ideas and laws about crimes are based.

Our first concern should be with an important concept—one that is bedrock to our freedoms. We are entitled to "due process of law" in our dealings with our governments. This concept has kept governments at bay and has preserved many of our civil rights.

A person accused of a crime is entitled to due process. The courts have interpreted this concept to consist of two components: *substantive* due process and *procedural* due process.

Substantive is about whether or not you did it. *Procedural* is about how the state must prove it and what can be done to you if the state succeeds.

Procedural due process is the stumbling block to better Dispute Management for criminal cases. The courts have construed this to mean that *adversary* trial methods must be used when the penalties are relatively severe.

It may be necessary to consider constitutional amendment to permit some of the options suggested in this chapter. I would hope not, as these would be options made available to the accused, or options which, if forced on an accused, would not result in the loss of liberty.

Other considerations and ideas about criminal justice must be understood. This short list covers the essentials:

- -all crimes are against the state, not the victim

- -the state, not the victim, has the exclusive right to accuse

- -the accused is assumed ("presumed," say the law books) to be innocent

- -the state must prove that the accused committed the crime

- -crimes are narrowly and precisely defined by statutes and precedents

- -the state must use "evidence" to prove that the accused committed the crime

- -"evidence" is narrowly, legally defined by codes of evidence and precedents

- -the proof must satisfy a jury that the accused is guilty "beyond a reasonable doubt"

- -proving guilt must happen in an adversary trial unless the accused admits guilt

Let's examine these ideas, one at a time. This will be essential to understanding what we can practically accomplish. It will leave some ideas for progress with criminal case dispute management in doubt.

We will conduct our examination in the context of a crime.

You come home from vacation to find your home normal enough, except for the broken window at the rear of the garage. You next see the door from the garage to the kitchen is ajar. When you enter the kitchen, you find a chaotic mess! It stinks—literally—as the refrigerator door has been left open for perhaps three or four days. Your TV is gone, as is your hi-fi equipment. Every room has been ransacked, and your files thrown on the floor. Clearly, the person who did this was looking for anything of value they could find.

The crowning blow came as you entered the master bathroom. They used it, but didn't flush it. You wonder if the police will find evidence here.

You call the police, and they come. They warn you that it is extremely unlikely that they will apprehend the person or persons who committed this crime against you.

Your neighbor, Ms. Simpson, solves the case. She recalls seeing a strange car parked up the street very early in the morning, perhaps two or three o'clock, several days ago. She is an elderly person and lives alone. She says it was one of those nights when she just couldn't sleep. With her binoculars, she was able to read the license tag and the make of the car.

A few days later the police call to tell you that two people were caught in the act of a residential burglary (the house had a silent alarm system) who were using the car identified by Ms. Simpson. Their fingerprints match the prints found in your home. They are arrested, charged, and out on bail. A public defender, paid by you and other taxpayers, is appointed to represent them. You resent the government subsidy granted to those in their line of work.

Now let's apply the basic legal principles listed above to your case:

-all crimes are against the state, not the victim

In Chapter One we discussed the need of rulers to retain power over government's formal dispute resolution processes. They knew that retaining power over the process of accusing and convicting alleged criminals was essential to control of the conquered. Out of such primitive needs for power grew our "justice" system.

Just as it was necessary to complain to the local royalty about a neighbor's sins against you, it is necessary to this day to complain to the police and prosecutor. They are the delegates of the "state" who can accuse and try the accused. You cannot drop by the courthouse, pay a filing fee, and accuse someone of a crime for which they could be fined, jailed or worse.

What a relief that is! When the penalty for commission of a crime is a fine or worse, this system is a protection for us all. The system works reasonably well in that we seldom hear people complain that someone wasn't *charged* with a crime, although we often hear complaints about how cases were handled.

The victim of a crime could file a civil suit, but civil courts have few remedies. Making someone say "I am sorry" and forcing them to clean up the mess they made while trashing your house is not within the power of a civil trial court.

Typically, they can do no more than enter a judgment for money damages. Then you have to spend still more money trying to collect it. This is a frustrating experience which will most likely increase your losses in the matter. In some states, a wage earner who is head of a household, has $50,000 of cash value in a life insurance policy and owns his own home is virtually untouchable by a creditor with a valid judgment! Even if you win your suit, you can't collect the money damages awarded to you. The defendants who harmed you have readily admitted to being penniless. Even their car did not belong to them; it was stolen.

How about modifying the system to permit use of other dispute resolution devices that do not require the victim to seek imprisonment of the accused, or a fine? How about adding some processes that would permit the victim to pursue other solutions with the accused?

-the state has the exclusive right to accuse

Getting the present criminal justice process started is difficult. You have to ask the prosecutor to initiate the process, and then the only process that he can initiate is a criminal prosecution, culminating in an adversary trial.[1]

---

1.   A few states permit "diversion" of an accused into non-adversarial processes, some of which include mediation processes. These are steps in the right direction.

Why not offer differing paths for victims? We could do so without depriving the state of the prerogative of initiating adversary proceedings against an offender.

If the victim feels that the appropriate action is to pursue heavy fines, imprisonment, or capital punishment, formal prosecution would remain the only path to these outcomes.

If the victim preferred another set of outcomes and the state (prosecutor) had no objection, why not permit use of other devices? They could be used in addition to the use of the normal criminal processes, or exclusively, should the prosecutor believe that appropriate.

-the accused is assumed ("presumed," say the lawbooks) to be innocent

Because of this assumption, the accused could under the present system thumb h/is/er nose at a victim when the prosecutor declined to use the adversary method.

If a victim can file a civil suit and force the offender to respond or risk a judgment, we should be able to do something here. Two ideas should be adopted.

First, we should accept the need to create a path that goes between the law's current simple offerings of only two paths, resolution—the civil courts and the criminal courts. Another path is needed. We could call the Third Path, "civil offense." It would be a hybrid of the existing legal ideas about civil trials on the one hand and criminal trials on the other. Why continue with only this simple dichotomy if it fails to provide a device and process we need?

In creating the new path, we would use many of the safeguards from civil cases that permit judges to take an early look at a case, even to conclude it when it is spurious. We don't want this path used by fake victims to victimize innocent people.

Once the judge was satisfied that the case was facially and substantially legitimate, the path could branch to use mediation, inquisitorial trial or several procedures in combination to explore pertinent relief for crime victims and the best approach to possible "rehabilitation" of offenders.

The new path must lead to more flexible remedies than are traditionally offered in the civil courts. Apologies, retractions, restitution, community service and other devices used by judges when giving criminals probation could as well be used as outcomes at the end of the Third Path. Something like probation supervision could be a remedy available in these proceedings. Could private companies provide the work?

-the state must prove the accused committed the crime

Third Path cases will still require proof of any essential fact that the accused is unwilling to admit. Admissions may be more likely in these proceedings as they cannot end with fines and jail.

By using inquisitorial proceedings, the judge will be able to guide both sides throughout the proceedings. The inquisitorial judge is free to raise issues, ask for specific evidence, and to suggest useful approaches to resolving the problem. This should keep costs lower, ensure appropriate use of appropriate proceedings at the right time, and tailor the outcome to the satisfaction of victim and accused.

In these proceedings, once the judge is satisfied that it is more likely than not that the accused committed the offense, the focus will change to what to do about it, and how to address any damage done to the victim. This won't be done by way of punishing the accused, but more to restore the victim—psychologically, as well as financially.

-crimes are narrowly and precisely defined by statutes and precedents

In Third Path proceedings, definitions *could* be looser and broader, but it wouldn't make sense to broaden them. Here's why.

We have a well-developed body of civil law and of criminal law. We probably have the waterfront of human behavior covered. What we are looking for in the Third Path is a different set of *processes* and *outcomes,* and *greater ease of proving things* than would otherwise apply in criminal cases.

So let's leave the definitions alone.

It makes sense not to identify classes of cases to be referred to Third Path. Third Path is appropriate for any case in which the victim wishes to pursue it. It is even possible that the prosecutor may pursue a full criminal conviction while Third Path is happening, though that is unlikely. I expect most prosecutors most of the time will operationally see Third Path as an alternative, not a parallel process.

-the state must use "evidence" to prove the accused committed the crime

At this point it is essential to explain the term "evidence."

When the trashing and theft occurred, and since, a great deal of *information* about the event and its consequences have accumulated. But information is not "evidence."

The *evidence* in a case is what is left of the *information* after the law's *rules of evidence* are applied to the information.

For example, still another neighbor may have told your son that she saw the two accused crawling through the garage window. The "hearsay" rule of evidence would not permit your son to repeat this information to the jury. Only the neighbor would be permitted to report this information.

In the inquisitorial trial used in our Third Path proceedings, there would be no jury. The judge would understand that serial communications, or "hearsay," are inherently unreliable as accurate sources of information. The judge might want confirmation from the neighbor, but might accept an affidavit instead of a live appearance. In a criminal trial, the accused has a "right of confrontation" that would forbid the use of such "evidence." We could lawfully permit such information when the outcome could not be a fine payable to the state, or imprisonment.

-"evidence" is narrowly, legally defined by codes of evidence and precedents

The evidence rules are the source of most of the "technicalities" that cause many of us to be outraged at court actions in some criminal cases.

Lawyers and judges contrive evidence rules for all the right reasons and for specific cases. That's the problem. Years later, the same rule will be applied in a different case and the result will seem crazy. It may *be* crazy! Lawyers and judges make abstractions of real events, and then decide the abstraction. The further they remove the lawsuit from the real-life events that brought it about, the more fantastic the version of the events presented at trial may seem.

When we consider the outcomes and inquisitorial processes of Third Path proceedings, we realize that these rules will be less important. They will be entirely unimportant in mediation proceedings involving these cases. There will be many cases in which our inquisitorial judges will order mediation of the dispute between the victim and the accused. If past experience with mediation is a guide, we can expect most of these cases to be resolved during or following mediation conferences.

-the proof must satisfy a jury that the accused is guilty "beyond a reasonable doubt"

The law permits proof by the "greater weight of the evidence" (that is, more likely true than not) in civil cases. In criminal cases, proof must be "beyond a reasonable doubt" (that is, true without a doubt for which I can state a logical reason).

Third Path cases are not criminal trials. The standard should be as simple as "more likely true than not," but could be as strict as "probably true." I'm not sure such fine distinctions matter to anyone but lawyers. A person is convinced or remains doubtful after hearing about a situation.

If the victim and the accused are able to agree on a solution during mediation, then proof is immaterial.

Should the judge have to decide the matter, we should expect that the remedies chosen by the judge will be less onerous in cases where the judge has more doubt and tougher when the judge feels reasonably certain s/he's right!

-proving guilt must happen in an adversary trial, unless the accused admits guilt

The Third Path doesn't lead to fines or jail. This is the key to escaping the adversary trial as the sole process for handling the kinds of cases we permit to go to Third Path. It can lead to repaying the victim for losses. A failure to do so after the judge orders it done could lead to jail, but only until payment is made. That's the way child support arrears are collected currently. When judges jail deadbeat dads, a phone call inevitably locates the money needed to pay child support.

An accused could admit guilt in a parallel criminal case and still be made a party to a Third Path case. The criminal courts might well await the outcome of Third Path proceedings before sentencing the accused to a fine, prison, or probation, and perhaps not adjudicating the accused to be guilty.[2]

How Can we do it?

Changing the criminal justice system will be a major challenge.

There is a flourishing and profitable business in prosecuting, defending, and judging criminals. Large populations of lawyers are entrenched here.

We must support the few judicial leaders who believe that approaches like our Third Path are not only feasible, but to be desired.

We must ask our legislative representatives for statutes enabling and requiring the processes required to make Third Path work. Third Path

---

2.   A "technicality" that permits the convicted party to retain civil rights otherwise lost on conviction of a felony.

cannot exist as a stand-alone process. It, like the processes we have generated for a new civil justice system, must be pursued as part of a system. The existing system must be modified for it to work constitutionally and effectively.

As you and I work toward the goal of an improved criminal justice system, we should keep a few things in mind.

Our civil rights are protected by the existing, adversarial system. We don't want to dismantle these vital protections. They protect us from the power of governments to unjustly and improperly accuse and prosecute. We want to make room for *additional* processes, not replace the existing safeguards.

High public profile cases are not going to be candidates for Third Path. Third Path is for the great majority of cases—those involving property crimes and minor personal offenses. Third Path is not for murders or other violent crimes. It isn't appropriate for criminal cases that have important social meaning. Third Path would not have been feasible for the Watergate, Rodney King or O.J. Simpson cases. Third Path will help with millions of cases, the kind you and I are likely to encounter. Traditional means—frustrating as they may sometimes be—are still best for serious criminal offenses and cases of wide public interest.

"Justice" is beyond us. Only God knows what is just. Justice for one human will seem unjust to some other human. We can rely on our court systems only for dispute resolution. At least that should be as good as we can make it.

10

Dispute Management for Private Organizations and Businesses

Governments don't think much about profits. Business people do. Businesses that are driven by market and consumer considerations have proven more profitable. America's business community has learned that quality counts heavily in keeping and gaining market share.

Non-profit, private organizations may not offer products for sale, but often offer services. Contributions and membership sales are enhanced by quality and appropriate positioning.

Both kinds of large organizations face similar populations of disputes. The obvious disputes with "outsiders": vendors, purchasers, regulatory agencies and the like. Less obvious, but increasingly important, are disputes *within* the organization. The most threatening of these come from employees and from labor legislation passed within the last ten years.

Quality control can only go so far. Its use is premised on the idea that with fewer defects in product and delivery of services, the organization will better achieve its financial and philosophical missions.

Even in the fully quality-controlled environment, bad things happen. What the organization does about them will distinguish organizations that use Dispute Management from those who do not. Dispute Management takes organizations beyond quality control.

Dispute Management assumes that disputes are variable, are inevitable, and that each dispute will be best resolved by choosing the proper process.

Using Dispute Management principles is pro-active. Failing to use them is to choose reactive management over pro-active management. If you fail to use Dispute Management principles consistently and continuously, you have chosen to send your organization's serious disputes to the traditional lawyer-court monopoly, with its attendant frustrations, costs, and delays.

You can dispose of a lawsuit more quickly and less expensively if you operate in states that have Florida-like modified court systems, but there are still better ways to manage disputes than heavy reliance on the courts and the bar.

Here's a modified set of Dispute Management Principles and a Dispute Management Work Order modified accordingly for use by private organizations:

The system will move adequate numbers of cases to resolution

The system will resolve cases quickly

The system will be simple enough that most people can use it without special assistance for the greatest possible numbers of cases

The system will emphasize redundancy of path and variety of method for dispute resolution

The system will move each case to the most appropriate dispute resolution path—to the simplest method likely to be effective for the dispute and its owners

The system will permit cases of possible concern for the culture of the organization, or having factual or legal precedential value to be identified and considered differently

The system will encourage and support the establishment of private dispute resolution: interpersonal, intra-organization and inter-organization

The system will handle disputes in-house when possible, then use private providers of dispute resolution services, and will be designed to keep disputes out of government channels unless other organization concerns dictate use of public courts

The system will, wherever feasible and to the extent consistent with the organization's mission, collect its cost from users

The system will gain feedback from all users, its providers and its managers

The system will continually self-adjust, based on management's responses

The costs of the system will remain proportionate to its continuing benefits as benefits are perceived by consumers, public, providers and managers

The Order of Work for implementing an organization's system will vary from that for a government, as would be expected:

Present and possible future consumers of dispute resolution services (in and out of the organization) will be identified

Demographic characteristics of populations of consumers will be related to the types of disputes of which they complain

Processes for dispute resolution will be identified and catalogued

Processes responding to consumer needs and demographics will be chosen

When should a dispute be allowed to go to court?

The process array will be established

Rules for both substantive and procedural aspects will be drafted and adopted

Management information systems will be designed and tested to assure adequate and continuous feedback of efficiency and attitudinal data to system managers

Management methods will be implemented to assure continuous and immediate correction within the system, as near as possible to the points of service delivery

Communication will be planned for system wide access to information about performance, modifications and needs.

Staffing begins
>Process managers will be chosen
>Service providers will be chosen

Training begins
>Process managers will be trained
>Service providers will be trained

Employees, purchasers of the organization's services and products and vendors will be informed about the system, and intake will begin

Feedback and response begin at the management level

Fine tuning begins—and never ends

Consumer, provider and management satisfaction measurement begins—and never ends

Fine-tuning and modification is the continuous response of the system to management data it generates

Let's create a company that could use Dispute Management to smooth its operations and reduce costs significantly.

ABC Construction, Inc., builds bridges in the eastern United States. They have a good business and are only partially debt financed. Debt increases as they take on new contracts, is lowered when final payment is received on a job.

The company has 135 full-time employees. Subcontractors are used on jobs to supplement the company's staff when the company is extremely busy. Labor is added and terminated as required by workload.

The business keeps its principal offices and yard at Baltimore. Each job site has an on-location office (a temporary trailer) for on-site management of the job. Executives and engineers travel to and from job sites primarily by automobile.

The company has suffered a litigation rate of 2.6 cases filed (by them or an adversary against them) for every ten million dollars of gross revenues. The average cost of direct expense of legal fees and court related costs has come to $27,500 per case.

The company wants to reduce the rate of filing by fifty percent and to reduce the cost per case by at least twenty-five percent. The company also asks the consultant to devise a way of limiting its exposure to large awards.

The cost of defense of some of the population of cases has been paid by insurance carriers. The premium is a proxy for the cost of indemnity and the cost of defense in these cases.

Outcomes have ranged from an adverse judgment of $75,000 (on appeal presently, awaiting the decision of the appellate court) to judgments favoring the company, as defense verdicts, and some judgments for damages awarded to the company. Most cases have been settled for small amounts of money paid out or received. Some of the payments and receipts have occurred after entry of judgment, and the consultant has considered the payment, not the judgment in these cases. The net outcome of all cases, in favor or and against the company for the study period, is a negative $6,250 in judgments.

The company expects annual gross revenues of $40 to $60 million. It has an internal rate of return of thirteen per cent. Taxable income is approximately six per cent of gross revenue.

The consultant advises the company that although outcomes can be made more rational and costs can be contained, there is no guarantee of outcome reduction when cases are tried in the state or federal court system or arbitrated in binding arbitration.

Now we'll use the modified Order of Work to analyze the company and suggest ideas for its Dispute Management program.

Present and possible future consumers of dispute resolution services will be identified

Working with a consultant, the company decides that its history shows these populations of potential litigants and other disputants (people with gripes, or with whom the organization has a gripe that aren't likely to go to court):

Contracting owners, typically government organizations (suits uncommon fewer than five per cent of the suits filed by or against the company)

Subcontractors hired by ABC (about sixty per cent of the suits filed by and against the company)

Employees, including short term, temporary, executive, and non-executive (increasing trouble here—only a few problems so far, but more on the way?)

Material and supply organizations (suits uncommon)

Operators of automobiles on roads used by employees (suits uncommon)

People who come onto premises being managed by the company and are injured (suits uncommon)

Demographic characteristics of populations of consumers will be related to the types of disputes of which they complain

The company and the contracting owners will probably have disputes over quality of work, design problems, payment, delays and order of work. Subcontractors and the company will have similar disputes. Employees are most likely to have disputes with the company over transfers, missed promotions, discrimination, disability, termination, and compensation. The company and its suppliers could have disputes over credit terms, payment, late deliveries, quality of deliveries and incorrect deliveries. Automobile accidents are a part of life for the company and its employees. There have been occasional claims for slipping and falling and the like outside the company's office in bad weather.

Processes for dispute resolution will be identified and catalogued

The consultant recommends consideration of conciliation training (to enhance managers inter-personal relationships with insiders and outsiders), negotiation training, mediation, peer review, and binding arbitration as possible components for use in a Dispute Management system.

Processes responding to consumer needs and demographics will be chosen

Owners, subcontractors, and suppliers could be provided with mediation and binding arbitration (for cases not settled by mediation) instead of resorting to the courts. Employees could be provided with a program of conciliation training, negotiation training, peer review (for disputes that could not become the subject of litigation, or are unlikely to), mediation and binding arbitration of all disputes not settled in mediation. The company is satisfied to let liability insurance carriers continue to manage premises and auto liability. The company's insurance policies cover the cost of lawyers for defense, as well as all court costs. The policies do not cover the company's direct and indirect costs of litigation in any other way. The policies require the cooperation of the company in preparing and presenting a defense to the claim. The consultant inquires to determine if the carriers encourage the use of mediation to gain earlier settlements of cases and how they go about it. This can save down-time for company employees and executives related to preparation for litigation and trials.

When should a dispute be allowed to go to court?

There are times when cash flows are extremely difficult for the company. At such times, delay in payment could be advantageous. The courts are notorious for slowing things down. Lawsuits can also be useful as power plays in negotiation with an economically less powerful adversary. The company decides to continue to rely on the courts in disputes with suppliers.

There are times when, and parties with whom, the company wishes to set a precedent, perhaps a factual one showing that the company will punish an executive who defects to a competitor in violation of an employment agreement. The company decides that all disputes over executive defection will be litigated or settled under threat of litigation. All other employee disputes will be handled by the new system. The contracts of employment used by the company will make it clear that all claims of employees concerning federally or state protected employment rights (e.g., sexual harassment, discrimination in promotion) will be handled by the new internal system.

The company's attorneys do not believe there are legal precedents to be set that will influence the course of the company's business. If there were, a means would have to be found to permit these cases to litigate in public courts, as they are the only source of legally binding precedent. They advise that with the agreement of the company and the adversary, any case can be exited from the new system to the courts.

The process array will be established
Rules for both substantive and procedural aspects will be drafted and adopted

The process array will consist of counseling and conciliation services, peer review panels and mediation and arbitration for employees, and mediation, arbitration and litigation for management of disputes with outsiders. Peer review will be limited to issues which management and the employee agree should not go to court. These agreements will be binding when made.

To deal with possible issues of corporate culture (not matters that could be litigated), any party could appeal a decision of a peer review board to the company's Board of Directors for a decision to be made by them in not more than thirty days. The Board of Directors would be permitted to substitute their decision for that of the peer review board in only this kind of case. Appeals to the Board from arbitrators' decisions about employee disputes would not be permitted except about non-legal matters of company culture.

The company's decisions have led to a process array that will differ, depending on which population of potential adversaries the company is addressing.

The consultant prepares a set of rules for the mediation process and another for the arbitration process. Working with the company's attorney, the consultant designs and represents the necessary language for the company's addenda to contracts with owners, clauses for contracts with subcontractors, agreements not to compete for executive level employees, employment agreements for all employees (including short term labor). Temporary service personnel are covered by their contracts with their employer, but the company attorney will review the contracts the company is signing to add these people to the workforce. The consultant will contact the temporary labor provider to encourage use of the company's system to resolve any conflicts the temps or their provider may have with the company.

Management information systems will be designed and tested to assure adequate and continuous feedback of efficiency and attitudinal data to system managers

With the consultant's help, simple sampling devices are created to measure all users' attitudes about the system and the efficiency of the system (time from inception to disposition, number of people who have to "touch" the problem, etc.). Responsibility for completion, collection, and analysis of the sampling instruments is assigned.

Management methods will be implemented to assure continuous and immediate correction within the system, as near as possible to the points of service delivery

Meetings of the team charged with operation and oversight of the system will be scheduled weekly for the first two months of the system's operation, then monthly thereafter. The consultant is asked to attend and facilitate these meetings as part of the initial training for employees. Immediate attention to unanticipated uses or misuse of the system is provided by full employee access to the team leader.

Communication will be planned for company-wide access to information about performance, modifications, and needs

As the attitudinal and performance evaluation information is accumulated, it will be reported to all employees in a brief newsletter. The letter will act as well to further the objective of explaining the system. Employees will be encouraged to bring disputes to the attention of a team member without delay. This may seem like asking for trouble, but a quick, appropriate and thorough response to a gripe may head off the deep anger that follows long-term frustration. People who can't get an answer from the company will go elsewhere to find it, probably a lawyer's office. Getting an answer in a fair and even-handed process and getting it quickly will meet most people's needs for respect and proper treatment.

Staffing begins
Process managers will be chosen

The consultant suggests that a team leader (the company decides its Human Resources Officer is the right person) and two members be chosen to manage the system. One will handle attitudinal data collection and processing. The other will monitor performance of the system. The leader will draft and publish the system newsletter and will handle all communications with the mediation and arbitration service provider. This should spread the load adequately.

Staffing begins
Service providers will be chosen

The consultant provides management with information about organizations providing dispute resolution in the Baltimore area. There are several organizations, some not-for-profit, others for profit. Their rates and policies have been compared by the consultant and reported to management. Management decides to use an organization that assures that all mediators have been trained extensively, are experienced and have experienced settlement rates in excess of seventy per cent of all cases mediated.

The organization will provide feedback and will see to it that the attitudinal and efficiency data is recorded and provided not less than weekly for the first two months of system operation, then monthly thereafter.

The organization agrees to provide a short list of former judges for use in arbitration, and to train the judges and mediators in the technical, business and economic environment in which the company operates.

To avoid delays in using the system, the rules adopted by the company delegate choice of a third party who is neutral (mediator or arbitrator) to the service provider. The provider enters a contract with the company setting out its rates and terms and agrees to take sole responsibility for collection of its fees from third parties in cases in which the company will only be paying its proportionate share (i.e., a dispute with a subcontractor).

Training begins
Process managers will be trained

The consultant provides a one day session for the team. They are introduced to the ideas of conciliation and negotiation, as well as oriented to mediation and arbitration.

Training begins
Service providers are trained

This step is eliminated, as the servicing organization has previously trained its third party neutrals.

Employees, purchasers of the organization's services and products, and vendors will be informed about the system and intake will begin

Employee orientation will take place in a series of training sessions. All employees will receive training in conciliation techniques and in negotiation. One day will be provided initially, and another day of negotiation training six months later, to avoid "training effect" phenomena and to correct misconceptions. New employees will receive the training program within six weeks of hiring. They will be given written information about the system upon hire and will interview with a Team member to ensure an adequate initial understanding of the system. During the first sessions, employees will learn how they can use the system, beginning with a talk with a team member, then continuing on to either peer review or mediation, and then to binding arbitration if no settlement results from mediation. Peer review is explained as a process in which other employees of the employee's rank will listen to the problem, consider it, then give their opinions about an appropriate outcome.

Simple rules are adopted for the peer review system, mediation, and arbitration of employee disputes. Easy access and counseling opportunities are assured. The peer review board is chosen by a vote of all employees and will serve for six months. Their decision is final on an issue and binding on the company and the employee. The board will consider issues that might be litigated and those that could not be litigated (i.e., disputes over access to company resources for work).

The other parties (for example, sub-contractors) the company has decided to cover with the system will be approached on an individual basis as need arises to contract with them with written descriptions of the system. They will be encouraged to agree, based on the mutual cost savings ensured by the system, the speed with which the system will operate, the simplicity of the system, and that all the third party mediators and arbitrators are unconnected with the company.

Feedback and response begin at the management level
Fine tuning begins—and never ends
Consumer, provider and management satisfaction
measurement begins, and never ends
Fine-tuning and modification is the continuous response of the
system to management data it generates

The team will ensure that these functions are accomplished. Collection and reporting of consumer and provider attitudinal information will be handled by the service provider. Internal satisfaction surveys will be undertaken at six-month intervals to monitor system success.

Does the company's system satisfy the demand of the Dispute Management Principles? Let's examine them:

The system will move adequate numbers of cases to resolution

All the disputes the company wished to refer to the system can be readily and promptly handled. The service provider ensures an adequate staff of neutrals and support staff to schedule each case within thirty days of notification of the dispute.

The system will resolve cases quickly

The rules recommended by the consultant ensure that no case can be pending for longer than six months. Most cases will be ended within ninety days.

The system will be simple enough that most people can use it without special assistance for the greatest possible numbers of cases

The company has provided both training and the team to assist employees in use of the system. The outsiders who will use the system will receive the assistance of the service provider in understanding and using the system. Outsiders would, of course, be free to employ attorneys to represent them in these proceedings.

Peer review and mediation require no legal or technical skills to use. Arbitration is slightly more complex, but the consultant's rules provide for guidance from the arbitrator for all parties to the dispute. These arbitrators are more like active, engaged "inquisitorial" judges than adversarial ones.

The system will emphasize redundancy of path and variety of method for dispute resolution
The system will move each case to the most appropriate dispute resolution path—to the simplest method likely to be effective for the dispute and its owners
The system will permit cases of possible concern for the culture of the organization or having factual or legal precedential value to be identified and considered differently

These Principles were satisfied during the planning and design stages. Depending on the group, a disputant or potential litigant will have conciliation and negotiation, the teams' services, mediation, peer review, and arbitration processes available. On a contract-by-contract basis with outsiders, the system can be used or withheld. If a deal involves creation of a useful legal precedent, the clauses invoking the system would not be used. If the possible legal or factual precedent could be harmful to the company, the system will be invoked by the contracts used in these relationships. Appeal from arbitration and peer review would address possible concerns with corporate culture and factual precedent for cases which all agree would not be litigated.

The system will encourage and support the establishment of private dispute resolution: interpersonal, intra-organization and inter-organization

The company's system establishes private resolution of disputes between the company, its employees, and selected outsiders. It encourages and supports the service provider—a private for profit organization—by using its services. It also encourages the use of better dispute management by its executives and other employees through the conciliation and negotiation training programs.

The system will handle disputes in-house when desirable, use private providers of dispute resolution services for cases that cannot be resolved in-house, and will be designed to keep disputes out of government channels unless other organization concerns dictate use of public courts

Mission accomplished!

The system will, wherever feasible and to the extent consistent with the organization's mission, collect its cost from users

The company will not ask employees to contribute to the cost of use of the system. The company will absorb all cost of initiation and continued management of the system. Outsiders (owner contractors, subcontractors) will pay their proportionate share of any required mediation and arbitration sessions. This allocation is equitable, as all involved will benefit by the system's use. Executive employees will pay their proportionate share of system use, should use of the system be mutually agreed upon, as opposed to the company's option to use the courts in these cases.

The system will gain feedback from all users, its providers, and its managers
The system will continually self-adjust, based on management's responses to information systems designed to assure dynamism and growth
The costs of the system will remain proportionate to its continuing benefits as benefits are perceived by consumers, public, providers and managers

The team will discharge these functions with the help of information furnished by the outside service provider. The team leader will report to the CEO and CFO to permit further evaluation of the cost savings of the system.

The company has taken the intelligent and utilitarian steps that comprise Dispute Management. It will reap the benefits of doing so.

Other organizations have taken up the work of becoming responsible for managing the population of disputes that are a necessary and unavoidable part of doing business.

E. I. Du Pont de Nemours and Company went to great lengths to gain control of the cost of the over four hundred law firms upon whom they relied for defense and offense. The company saved millions the first year. This company, like Ford Motor Company, is finding effective solutions to disputes in mediation.

Construction giant Brown and Root was concerned with the company's exposure to jury verdicts in employee lawsuits for alleged employment law violations. The company created an internal dispute resolution system, employing mediation and arbitration and using a third party dispute resolution organization. As a benefit to employees, they will pay $2,500 to the employee's lawyer to permit the employee to use the services of an attorney in the system. The attorney is limited to charging the employee no more than the fee to be paid by Brown and Root. Even paying employee's lawyers to present disputes, Brown and Root calculate their savings in the millions over the usual costs of managing these disputes!

Small companies profit from Dispute Management as well. A small building contractor has completely avoided lawsuits from dissatisfied consumers of homes. It has improved consumer attitudes about the company by establishing a company-paid program of mediation and fast-track arbitration for consumer complaints. In over three years of use, only two cases have required arbitration. All the rest settled with an agreement between homeowner and contractor—accomplished at mediation.

What organizations can profit from Dispute Management methods? Only those that sell and buy products and services or which have employees!

11

Dispute Management for You—Taking Charge

What do you do when faced with a dispute?

The ancient choice was to fight or flee. Seek victory (and risk defeat) or retreat.

One could also choose to ignore the stimulus to dispute by turning the other cheek or just looking away.

Ancient peoples had other ways of dealing with disputes. Imagine a small group of early humans: hunters, gatherers, scavengers for food. They had no "home" and they had not yet discovered agriculture. They were nomads, traveling their territory in small groups.

In our imaginary troupe we find eleven people. Two of the eleven are large, powerful young males. They are the sons of an older female who remains able to travel with the group.

A dispute arises between the two young males over who will mate with one of the young females. They pick up weapons, but before a blow can be landed they find their mother standing between them, insisting that they talk with her, reason with her. She hears both their complaints and claims. She separates them to talk privately to each.

Her wisdom leads her to believe that this is no dispute over love. She thinks the fight over the younger female has been chosen as a vehicle to decide who will lead the group. The younger brother is clearly challenging the older. If he wins the combat for the female, he wins the combat for leadership. The conflict is symbolic.

The older brother has been canny and able in finding game and in devising both aggressive and defensive strategies and tactics with which the group has both gained and defended territory.

The younger brother is stronger and faster—a better fighter. He will probably win if there is a combat. It is certain that each of these men will seriously wound the other before the fight is done.

The elder female proposes that the older brother become a shaman, the wise man whose advice all must seek, including the chief. No move can be made until the shaman and the chief agree if it involves the safety of the troupe. If a deadlock occurs, mother will intervene, and if necessary vote to break the tie.

She suggests that younger brother will become chief. He has years in which to mate, and older brother should mate with the younger female who was the ostensible cause and object of the dispute. Older brother will be a patient father, less likely to be lost in hunting or battle accidents. He will more likely be present to help rear the children.

The brothers agree. The young woman agrees. She would be honored by either outcome and given high status in the group. Her children will receive special treatment as well. This way she doesn't have the risk that both suitable mates could die from wounds received in their combat. The troupe agrees, as this outcome preserves the resources that the young males represent and stops a disturbing confrontation.

Conciliation and negotiation (what Mom did with both her boys) as part of the process of mediation (what Mom, the younger female, the boys and the troupe members engaged in with Mom's services as mediator) predates written history. By Hammurabi's time some four thousand years ago, these processes were already well known to humans. By the time of "civilization," people had settled into communities, agriculture and trade had been discovered, and rulers were using power-based methods to control their subjects. The adversary process was in place long before Hammarabi's reign.

In communities all over the world, negotiation and mediation were practiced on a daily basis. These most ancient ways of addressing human disputes are also the most preferred ways. No matter the ethnic group a person claimed to belong to, they first preferred negotiation to settle a dispute, then mediation, if negotiation efforts failed to resolve the problem.

A distant next choice was one of the forms of adjudication—arbitration or trial.

So why have all governments provided only adjudication systems, such as the Anglo-American courts? Because of the desire of those in control of governments to control the people they rule. (We discussed this in Chapter 4, "How We Got This Way.")

The Norman Kings of England understood the insanity (in their system) of permitting the newly conquered to have run their own "courts." The power to decide disputes between the barons was also of critical importance to the king. Courts were created over time from members of the king's court who could be trusted to carry out royal policy. Letting people make their own law and rules, as would happen in a system based on negotiation and mediation, was not consistent with the interest of the monarch in maintaining political and practical control of the wealth of the land.

The power to decide others "rights" has been jealously guarded by governments for millennia, but that doesn't mean that governments totally succeeded. In Eastern Asia in particular, resort to the courts caused a loss of face and prestige. There "real people" negotiated their disputes and used trusted mediators to help with disputes they couldn't resolve.

In my travels around the globe, I have found that some people negotiate more and with more skill than others. Many Europeans, British, and North Americans, and people from places populated by migrants from these areas seem disinclined to negotiate on a daily basis.

What was my first clue? I have tried to negotiate with people everywhere. I was often rebuffed in Northern Europe and the other areas I noted. Everywhere else, my efforts were met with a smile. "At last!" they said. "An American who understands!"

In most of the world it is rude to fail to negotiate, whereas in our parts of the world merchants have convinced us that it is rude to negotiate.

In our country we have, until recently, relied upon a governmental system using only the adversarial trial as the method of dispute resolution. We negotiated what we could, but we seemed to have forgotten mediation. Its formal re-discovery began in the late sixties with the "alternative life style" movement. It was independently rediscovered in the seventies by Al Coogler, an Atlanta attorney who saw that a method of mediation could help couples resolve issues in divorce cases. He went on to conceive the Academy of Family Mediators.

It was re-discovered in Florida over the sixteen years from my 1972 monograph through the mid-eighties.

Dispute Management will help you break free from the unfortunate assumptions that lead us to think that fighting, fleeing or going to court are the only alternatives for handling difficult disputes.

An individual will use Dispute Management to take charge of every possible aspect of the disputes s/he expects to encounter and to be prepared for those not anticipated. It means developing personal dispute resolution skills and getting the people you live with, work with and deal with to do the same thing.

You will anticipate as many disputes as you can and will be prepared to deal with them, with newly acquired interpersonal skills. In those rare cases when conciliation and negotiation don't end the problem, you will use mediation and fast-track arbitration, the least expensive means of third party dispute resolution available. It means learning how *little* you must use lawyers and traditional courts. You will learn to use lawyers to avoid using lawyers!

What can you do about your disputes? Begin by learning about conciliation and negotiation skills. Next, take a course in mediation skills.

Then practice, practice, practice! We can catch up with the rest of the world if we work at it!

Conciliation is the act or the acts of finding ways to reconcile differences. It is peacemaking, friend-making, friend-keeping work. Once you begin to ask for something, you have moved to negotiation. To learn about conciliation, find literature that deals with making others comfortable emotionally. Counseling and therapy literature often talk about creating an environment in which the patient is put at ease. Perhaps you know someone special. Being around this person is like taking a tranquilizer! S/he makes you feel relaxed and pleasant. Start thinking about how s/he does it. Ask this person how they do it! You may already be good at this, and may skip this step.

To sharpen negotiation skills (or begin learning, as the case may be for you), I can recommend three books. Start with Herb Cohen's *You Can Negotiate Anything..*." It is light-hearted, filled with useful advice, and will give you self-confidence.

Next, read Fisher and Ury's *Getting to Yes*, now in its second edition. It is a book about methods of principled negotiation, not tricks of the trade. Their method is the method I use when I am working as a mediator, negotiating for and with all sides of a dispute. I have never had anyone tell me that I engaged in any conduct which was inappropriate, but I have helped many, many people and organizations end disputes by accepting settlements defined through mediation.

Finally, take an "encyclopedic" approach to negotiation. Read George Fuller's *Negotiator's Handbook*. This is a book filled with checklists. You can even find the negotiation ploy—"good cop, bad cop"—in the index! Fuller suggests many "do's and don'ts" for negotiators. If you like more rigid rules than Fisher and Ury provide, you will find them here. Roger Dawson's *Secrets of Power Negotiating* rounds out your introductory reading.

Take the time to take a course in negotiation. In addition to one exploring theory, practice, and ethics, you will want a course that lets you simulate negotiations, then holds round-table critiques. Pick a course with a faculty that actually negotiates for a living, not one that *talks about* negotiation for a living. Ask for the names and telephone numbers of all the people who took their last course and for whom they last worked as negotiators. If the providers of the course permit participants to evaluate the course, ask for copies of the evaluations. If they don't permit and encourage their audiences to evaluate them or won't share the evaluations with you, move on to the next provider. Try to negotiate a better price with the people who offer the course. Surely they of all people should respond good-naturedly.

A course in mediation skills is your next step. If you enjoy helping others, learning to be a mediator will be one of the most rewarding experiences of your lifetime. Look for the same information and characteristics I thought important in a negotiation course. Be prepared to spend up to five days in this course. Remember, mediation is an enhanced and assisted form of negotiation. It is a more complex subject, building on an understanding of the negotiation process. Good mediation courses will teach you about negotiation as well, but not as thoroughly as a course devoted to negotiation skills.

Good negotiation and mediation courses will spend time developing conciliation skills, as relationship-building skills are essential to negotiation and mediation. Every effective sales person knows that the first job is to establish a positive relationship with the prospect. The second job is to maintain that relationship. Conciliation training will help you to learn more of how this vital work is accomplished.

These courses are offered at Harvard, through the National Institute for Trial Advocacy, and at many universities and Continuing Education facilities nationwide. My company, Dispute Management, Inc., offers the courses at its Orlando, Florida offices and in other states as well. It will encourage you to learn that my best customers are lawyers looking for ways to better serve their clients' needs.

To their credit, lawyers have shown a great interest in these courses and have encouraged the growth of the mediator training industry.

Call lawyers you know for recommendations and leads to good courses.

If you haven't the time or the money for the courses, read *The Mediation Process* by Dr. Christopher Moore. This thoughtful book will give you an excellent orientation to the work of the mediator and the dynamics of mediating.

Once you finish your education in negotiation and mediation, go do it! Better still, start practicing negotiation and mediation skills as soon as you have learned just a little. As a human being, you already know a lot about this; you just haven't organized your thinking about these subjects, and you have no body of experience. Get started now in gaining that experience. In the long run, it will be more important than the course you take, although the latter will accelerate the coming of the day you feel comfortable as a good negotiator.

Become aware of what you can and cannot negotiate. Trying to get a discount on bulk purchases of postage stamps will be frustrating. Getting a better price for a toner cartridge will more likely be successful.

Picking your time and place will matter. The salesperson in the upscale store may be on commission, it may be the end of the month, there might be a sales contest going on, or bonuses to be made by increasing sales, but if you try to haggle with other customers as an audience, you are more likely to fail. Buy a blouse, then take the sales person aside and offer to buy two more if you can get thirty percent off on the lot. If they come back with only ten percent off, go for twenty and close your deal!

Now that you have built a base upon which you can apply them, apply the Dispute Management Principles. For your personal use, we need to restate them. I'll state the Principle first, then the restatement for personal use:

> *The system will move adequate numbers of cases to resolution*
>   I am going to have a plan for every kind of dispute I may
>   have

The system will resolve cases quickly
> I will try to get disputes over with quickly, not let them linger

The system will emphasize redundancy of path and variety of method for dispute resolution

The system will move each case to the most appropriate dispute resolution path to the simplest method likely to be effective for the dispute and its owners

The system will permit cases of possible social concern or precedential value to be identified and considered differently

The system will encourage and support the establishment of private dispute resolution: interpersonal, intra-organization and inter-organization

The system will move cases that can be handled privately into private dispute resolution, and out of government channels

I'll work full time at maintaining good relationships with the people I deal with—at home, as well as at the office. I will be a principled negotiator. I will negotiate about as many things as I can. I will use the services of a trained mediator when an issue that really matters can't be resolved through negotiation. If mediation doesn't help, I'll use fast-track arbitration rather than go to court. I will use a lawyer only in situations that are financially threatening when the cost may be justified. When I use a lawyer, I'll use them only to the extent I really need to. I'll get information from them and use them as a resource, not as my delegates. I won't take the easy way out and just dump the problem in the lawyer's lap. I'll read the contracts I am asked to sign to see if I am dealing with a business that has thought about Dispute Management. I'll find clauses dealing with mediation and arbitration if I am. If they aren't there, I will ask that they be added. I will start to negotiate with my children. I know I have the power to give them orders, but how will they ever learn better ways if I don't start this at home?

The system will, wherever feasible and to the extent possible, collect its cost from users

When I go into a business or financial deal, I'll remember to include clauses in the contracts and agreements that require disputes to be mediated, then arbitrated if mediation does not produce a settlement. We can use a company that has rules dividing the fees between the disputants and which provides its office facilities, personnel and a rule structure for the process. That way I don't have to write so much into the deal. (See Appendix A for a sample clause, and Appendix B and C for sample company rules for mediation and arbitration, respectively.)

The system will gain feedback from consumers, the public, its providers and its managers
The system will continually self-adjust, based on management's responses to information systems designed to assure dynamism and growth
The costs of the system will remain proportionate to its continuing benefits, as benefits are perceived by consumers, public, providers and managers

I know I will learn more about my system by applying the Dispute Management Principles. I know that negotiating more and more skillfully cannot hurt. I'll have to watch to see if I have missed opportunities to use mediation services, or perhaps have had disputes which I could have negotiated on my own—with patience—and saved the cost of the mediator. If I have records of costs of other disputes handled in the traditional ways of courts and lawyers, I will compare the costs of my new system to them. I will expect to see a savings.

The next step, the Dispute Management order of work, will be much simpler for you. You have planned your personal preparation through reading and courses. You have begun to practice negotiation and mediation in your personal and business life. Reorganizing a government court system or creating a system for an organization is far more complicated than the work you will do to complete your personal system and begin its operations.

Here's a possible Order of Work for you:

You want to locate people who can provide mediation and arbitration services in your community. After you have completed your reading and taken the courses, you will know better what you are looking for. Write down the criteria of greatest importance to you.

Locate providers of dispute resolution services. Ask lawyers you know, look in the yellow pages, try the internet and, if the local court system uses mediation, get some leads there. Talk to individuals from profit organizations and non-profit organizations. Interview the providers—not just the administrators, but the people who will actually provide the service. As in any other work, some individuals excel, while others will leave you wondering.

You may find the interest and level of service of the for-profit organizations to be superior to the non-profits. Most are strongly oriented toward you, the consumer. They are market-driven organizations. The non-profit may deliver high levels of service if you deliver significant contributions. The for-profit needs you to stay in business. It is not receiving annual donations from major foundations to cover losses and financial inefficiencies.

Obtain copies of the organization's rules and suggested clauses for inclusion in your important written contracts with others.[1] Be sure the processes used by the organization are simple and readily understandable. One of your objectives is to avoid the expense of having to use a lawyer to get something decided. Complex procedures require legal advice.

Be sure you understand how they charge. Some will want "administrative fees" to open a file. Most will charge for the hours taken to mediate or arbitrate. Some will have cancellation fees and minimum fees for cases. Some charge based on the amount involved (stay away from these for your financially important cases, at least). Negotiate a

---

1.   See Appendix A for a sample.

fee schedule that will work for you. The best time to do this is when you actually have a dispute and the provider knows that saying "yes" will bring cash flow in the near future.

Talk to friends and colleagues about working with you in a cooperative group to provide mediation and arbitration for each other. There are disputes which are important but which do not justify the cost of a dispute resolution provider's services. Within your church, social and business associations, and circle of friends you will find people interested in better management of their disputes. Perhaps you can hire a trainer for one of these groups, with everyone chipping in to pay for the trainer's time.

Even if you don't need a lawyer now, begin the process of finding lawyers that are knowledgeable about the subjects you might need help with. Some states have certification processes for lawyers which require passing rigorous exams and require demonstrated experience in a field. Although no assurance that the lawyer is actually good at the certified area, it's a start. Satisfied clients are an even better source of leads. If your peers have been satisfied in long-term relationships with an attorney, that bodes well for the lawyer involved.

Interview the lawyers you have picked. You want to end up with someone who is knowledgeable about estates, taxes, probate and administration of estates and property law; as well as another who knows how to successfully litigate the kinds of cases you think you might have. Have them tell you how they charge, and get it in writing. Some lawyers have a general "engagement" letter that spells out their relationship with you. If you don't understand it, ask for a better letter. If you don't like some of the terms, negotiate them!

Make sure the lawyers you use are committed to the use of mediation and binding arbitration as a means of resolving disputes. If they balk, beware! The use of the courts will be significantly more expensive than using so-called "alternative dispute resolution" (the phrase lawyers like to use to describe conciliation, mediation and arbitration).[2] Discuss your use of a private dispute resolution provider. Get their suggestions for which mediators and arbitrators they think do the best work. Talk to the organizations that employ these people, if you've not already done so.

You will encounter lawyers who support your effort to use mediation, but will suggest that it works much better if you file a lawsuit first. Of course they will! A law-suit is a tar baby. Once you touch it, you will find it hard to get free again, and impossible to do without your lawyer's help. If the other side files a counterclaim, then even if you dismiss your claim against them, their claim against you can go on to trial.

It is true that mediation of some claims is more effective after litigation has been commenced and legal discovery has occurred. Talk to the dispute resolution service provider—a good one can help you make the decision of mediating now or later or both. They will want to help you end the dispute as soon as possible. They have no economic interest in keeping the file on your case open for months at a time. They are only paid when they work at mediation and arbitration.

Another group of lawyers will say mediation is fine, but they never arbitrate. These lawyers believe that all arbitration is as slow as court litigation and costs about the same. Their advice is well-intentioned, but based on an erroneous assumption. The assumption is that all arbitrations are conducted the same way.

Arbitration happens only when you have contracted for it, and you can ask to know the terms of a contract before you sign it. If it calls for arbitration according to the rules of an organization, get the rules and read them before you sign. If their rules permit the parties to pick an arbitrator, it will slow the process. If the rules permit "discovery" depositions or the like, it will slow the process and increase your cost. The rules should provide short periods of time for every event. They should

---

2.   Most cases are settled by negotiation and mediation. Even in states with the old system, fewer than six per cent of all filed cases ever go to trial. Isn't trial the "alternative" dispute resolution method?

provide for a reasoned, articulated decision of the arbitrator within a short period of time after completion of the arbitration proceeding.[3]

If your lawyer complains that there is no appeal from arbitration, she's right, but ask them how many cases they appeal anyway. One out of one hundred? If it's more than that, why are they losing so many cases? If your lawyer's concern is that the arbitrator may make a decision on some basis other than what the law requires, then contract with the service provider that the law will be applied and ask for a review of disputed decisions by the service provider. If they agree that the law was not applied, it's back for another arbitration *with another arbitrator.*

It's still cheaper than a trial, a bad result and an appeal. Litigation costs for a case can range from perhaps $5,000 to well over $100,000 for routine litigation. Add a twist or two, as in patent infringement, and the cost can be over $500,000! For one side!

A one day arbitration or mediation conducted by you and your adversary, with a trained third party (many organizations will provide a respected former or retired trial judge for this work, at no additional charge) will cost you from $1,000 to perhaps $3500, if you shop.

By the way, lower prices don't necessarily signal lower quality in the dispute resolution field. Overhead is lower for these professionals than that for operating a law office. They can choose to pass the savings on to you. Of course high demand or a neutral's wish to only be employed in high stakes cases can result in higher hourly rates for that person's services.

You can use a lawyer as a resource of knowledge when mediating and arbitrating. Expect to pay for about one day's work to let the lawyer prepare, and for another day's work at the mediation or arbitration conference. Let the lawyer know that you are not looking to them to take responsibility for the outcome, only to provide you with information and "coaching." Having a lawyer handy when the other side has

---

3. Take a look at the arbitration rules in appendix C. They demonstrate just how fast and simple arbitration can be.

chosen to use one or when you are dealing with a legally complex idea is comforting.

To bring about long-term change, we need to ask for our children's help. We need to begin the process of educating them about conciliation, negotiation and mediation. We need to give them practice opportunities. "Because I said so!" cuts off negotiation. There will be times for parents to use power, but let's keep them to a minimum.

Public schools have begun to teach children about dispute resolution skills. In some school systems in Massachusetts and in Florida, school children and young adults are mediating for each other. They have received special training and are accepted by their peers as people who can help. What outstanding preparation for the future, for both the mediators and those receiving their services!

If our children can learn of the ancient ways and modern applications of conciliation, negotiation, and mediation, will it change their world? Presently, we live in a culture that makes a fist when frustrated. If more of us understood the old skills, perhaps frustration would provoke nothing more than the proffer of an open hand and a friendly, "Can we talk?"

Managing our lives gives us feelings of confidence and competence. We are no less able to manage the disputes that come our way than the other facets of our lives. We simply need to prepare for them and to have a plan. Dispute Management provides the planning tools.

12

From Here To Where?

You know your powers, your capabilities, and what you are willing to do to improve dispute resolution in your community, your business and in our country.

If you do no more than personal Dispute Management, that will be important.

If you are a business leader or are charged with responsibility for the disputes your company encounters, there is much you can do. You can hire a consultant, become better educated about dispute resolution processes and techniques, and begin to lobby for better ways of handling in-house and outside disputes.

If you are a government official, the sky is the limit! There are millions of people in desperate need of quicker, simpler and cheaper dispute resolution. This book shows how one state helped its people, and how people like me and you hope for still more improvements.

If you are a judge or a court administrator, there is specialized and knowledgeable help available. Consultants like me and other people who make up institutions such as the State Justice Institute, the National Institute for Dispute Resolution, and the National Center for State Courts are just a few of the Americans accumulating knowledge about better ways to organize and run a state court system. Get on board!

Want to change major systems permanently? If you are an educator, help America's children learn about Dispute Management. Start them with basic dispute resolution skills and give them a chance to practice them. Reward the kids that use these skills. Encourage their peers to emulate them.

These are exciting times. Americans are just now beginning to take responsibility for managing their disputes. Please, please join me in making it happen!

Appendices

Appendix A

Rules for Mediation

❖

(Courtesy of Dispute Management, Inc., DeLand, Florida. www.dispute-management.com)

INTRODUCTION

The Rules for DMI's mediations have been crafted to keep the process as simple and as speedy as those involved can make it. Unless all parties agree to a modification of these Rules or to the selection of any option mentioned below, each of the "Rules" is binding. If you select an option in writing or agree to an amendment of the Rules, again in writing, and all parties sign the agreement and forward it to DMI, DMI will abide by the choice and conduct itself accordingly. DMI reserves the right not to permit amendment to the Rules, should the amendment have any economic impact on DMI's operations or on the operations of the mediator.

THE AGREEMENT TO MEDIATE

When you have agreed to mediate according to DMI's Rules, these are the rules you will be following.

Such an agreement can occur in advance of disputes, as in a written contract to purchase or sell, or provide some service in which it is agreed that disputes will be handled according to Dispute Management's Rules

You could also agree, after a dispute has come about, to handle your dispute through mediation, perhaps coupled with arbitration, should mediation not produce a settlement. This choice assures that the dispute will be handled to a binding and enforceable conclusion by the least expensive and quickest method if you also make it clear that mediation and arbitration will be conducted only according to DMI's published rules. Other organizations and individual neutrals won't be following DMI's special, rapid and less expensive systems.

STARTING MEDIATION

Three situations are likely.

First, you may have agreed, in a written contract, to mediate any disputes arising in connection with the contract or some other transaction. In this case, if either of the parties notifies DMI in writing of the desire to mediate a dispute, stating simply the nature of the dispute and the names, addresses, and telephone numbers of the opposing parties, DMI will begin the process of setting a hearing time, choosing a mediator or mediators, and giving appropriate written notice to all concerned.

Two, it's possible that an agreement has been reached, orally or in writing, since the contract was entered. Often parties wishing to control the cost of disputes and to better manage them to a swift conclusion will agree to mediate a dispute rather than permit it to fall into the courts and litigation. DMI will respond to your written or oral request for mediation exactly as if you had agreed to mediation in your original contract.

Three, it's possible that you don't know whether the other party will agree to mediation or not. If you call us or write us, telling us about the dispute and giving us the name, address, and telephone number of the other parties, we'll contact them to see if they will agree to a quicker, less expensive process of dispute resolution. If they do, we'll notify you, prepare a simple agreement incorporating these mediation rules (unless you or an attorney would prefer to do this), then we will proceed with the selection of a mediator (or when especially requested more than one mediator), and setting the time for the hearing.

APPOINTMENT OF THE MEDIATOR

If you've signed a contract or other document which provides that mediation will take place according to the Rules of Dispute Management, Inc. as presently published, DMI will select a mediator qualified to preside over your mediation hearing. The mediator will be a lawyer with experience about the subject of the dispute. Some mediators are former judges and can be especially requested. If either party requests a former judge, DMI will assign one unless the other party objects to any additional cost which might be charged by the former judge, in which case DMI will appoint an attorney mediator at a lower rate. Objections to the appointment of a mediator and requests for the appointment of a judicial mediator must be filed with DMI within five days of receiving notice of the mediation. Please call DMI if you want to know more about the mediator appointed to your case. Each party is entitled to reject one mediator, without stating any reasons for the rejection. DMI will immediately appoint another mediator, according to these Rules.

Mediators' fees vary with their experience. Additionally, some mediators charge for their travel time and expenses as well as for meals and lodging while away from home on mediation business.

DMI keeps track of the various charges made by mediators working through DMI. If you request, we will provide the categories of charges to you in advance, so you will be aware of what charges might be incurred with the use of any mediator.

Once a mediator has been selected, we will provide you with any resumé information we have on the mediator so you can know more about this person before meeting him/her during the proceedings.

USING LAWYERS IN MEDIATION

We encourage you to use the services of a lawyer during mediation, and in preparation for mediation. However, our mediators have ample experience with dispute resolution processes, and lawyers are not required to let you use the system. The additional cost of a lawyer may not be required or desirable to the parties. We do not require that anyone have a lawyer, but if one of the parties employs a lawyer, the other party or parties should seriously consider doing so as well. Lawyers have detailed and specialized knowledge about dispute resolution and can be extremely helpful in resolving disputes. Mediators are not permitted to give legal advice, but can provide limited information about the law.

Since there are no rules of evidence or procedure or "traps" to worry about in mediated proceedings, you may choose to attend without a lawyer. If you do so, DMI's mediators, as well as DMI, join in encouraging you to use the services of a lawyer in evaluating any agreement reached during mediation before it becomes final and binding. Agreements can be reached "in principle" which are clearly stated not to be binding upon any party until the parties and their attorneys have signed the documents to signify their approval. DMI's mediators will be glad to show you how that can be done.

WITNESSES

You won't need to go to the expense of bringing your witnesses to mediation. If you'd like, you can have them write out statements about what information they would give if they came. Or, you can simply tell the mediator what they have told you.

There's no examination or cross-examination of anyone, including any witnesses, during a DMI mediation. You can read DMI's publication, "What Is Mediation?" for more information about the process itself.

SETTING THE MEDIATION CONFERENCE

DMI will set the date, time, and the place of each mediation session. We will endeavor to set a time, date, and place that is mutually agreeable to all parties and their attorneys. However, if after five business days of effort to find a mutually acceptable time, date, and place, this cannot be accomplished by DMI, then DMI will set a date not less than sixty days from the date on which the effort to find a hearing date commenced. This date, time, and place will be as binding upon the parties as if agreed to by them in writing.

CANCELLATIONS AND POSTPONEMENTS OF HEARINGS

When mediation dates and times are reserved, you are not buying an "option" on the mediator's time and DMI's resources, which you may choose to exercise or not. You are actually buying the committed date and hours for the hearing and the mediator's commitment to be there for the time and on the date reserved. When you reserve your date and time, DMI has committed its resources to your mediation during the period of time you have requested.

When a mediation conference date and time is scheduled, the mediator is 100% committed to being present, barring acts of nature, serious illness or death. The mediator or mediators are not permitted to accept other work for this time period.

If you should cancel your mediation more than thirty days before the hearing, with the agreement of all parties, there will be no charge for the reserved time, except that DMI will retain the amounts paid for administration fees. The balance paid DMI will be refunded.

If you cancel or postpone within thirty days of the committed hearing time and DMI is able to find other arbitration or mediation work for the mediator for all or a part of the reserved time period, then to the extent other work is found there will be no charge for the committed time. To the extent DMI is unable to replace the committed work with new work, you will be invoiced for the difference. DMI will retain all sums paid as administration fees.

When a cancellation or postponement occurs and an additional hearing is requested, the party (if one party's emergency brings about a cancellation or postponement) or the parties (when all parties have agreed to a cancellation or postponement) will deposit with DMI the additional total sum of $150.00 to cover DMI's additional costs for further processing of the case.

Once all parties have agreed to a mediation time, date, and place, DMI will not change it unless all parties agree to the change. Please agree to these terms with care, and be sure your schedule is free for the time and date.

PRE-CONFERENCE MEMORANDA

You will have to decide whether it would be helpful to the mediator and to others involved in the dispute to have a written understanding of how you see things. If you do, you're welcome to provide such a document to the mediator and to the other parties in advance of the mediation conference.

Because mediators do not make decisions that are binding on you, it is perfectly all right for you to submit documents, in confidence, to the mediator before the session. Our mediators are trained not to be influenced by any private communication, only to be informed by them. However, we realize that you may wish to give information to the mediator as you would during one of the private conferences in a mediation session, but in advance of the conference date. This is perfectly permissible.

DMI will invoice you for the time required by the mediator to review the materials you submit.

CONDUCT OF THE MEDIATOR

DMI's mediators will conduct themselves according to the standards of conduct adopted for court certified mediators in Florida. These standards are published by the Supreme Court of Florida.

DMI's mediators will conduct mediations according to the Florida Rules of Civil Procedure except when those Rules conflict with these Rules, in which case these Rules will govern.

By following published standards and Rules we can assure due process and an effective mediation to all those who bring disputes to us for mediation.

OUR HEARINGS ARE CONFIDENTIAL

Hearings and conferences which are conducted by DMI are closed to the public. They are private, confidential proceedings, to be attended only by the disputants and parties, their attorneys, and any other trusted experts and advisors. All parties and their attorneys, by using these DMI dispute resolution processes, agree unconditionally that the mediator will not be subpoenaed or summonsed for any purpose nor at any time be required to testify concerning the proceedings.

No party or other person attending the mediation session will testify about any communication made during such hearing or any communication between that party or person and the mediator.

No one will make any recording or stenographic record of the conference or hearing. Note taking during the proceedings is permitted, but no verbatim or semi-verbatim records shall be made by any person.

All parties agree, by using a DMI dispute resolution process, that DMI is not a necessary or proper party in any proceedings—judicial, or administrative—relating to the dispute resolution process, nor shall DMI or any mediator operating for DMI in these proceedings be liable for any act or omission to act in connection with the conduct of mediation pursuant to these Rules.

WHEN YOU DON'T UNDERSTAND WHAT A RULE MEANS

When your question involves the conduct of the mediation conference, then the mediator will be the sole and final judge of the meaning of the Rule, subject only to appeal to the President of Dispute Management, Inc.

If the problem arises in the administration of mediation, other than in the actual conduct of the mediation conference and what goes on when the parties are meeting together, then DMI will be the sole and final judge of what should be done.

THINGS WE DON'T CHARGE FOR

We don't charge for the use of any of our office machines, telephone services, other facilities, or personnel when used in reasonable ways in conjunction with facilitating the mediation.

SOME OTHER THINGS WE CHARGE FOR

We reserve the right to make reasonable and customary business charges for long copy runs, long distance telephone calls made at your request, FAX transmissions and receipts made for your convenience, and for any costs we advance for you or your hearing (such as requested projectors, screens or other equipment you especially ask for).

HOW DMI IS PAID

When you request a mediation, you will need to send DMI funds equal to your share of a minimum of four hours of mediation ($75 an hour up to $125 an hour for each party in a two party case, depending on the mediator you choose), plus a non-refundable administration fee of $250.00. Excepting the administration fee, we will hold this money in escrow until it has been earned according to the terms of these rules.

We will collect a similar sum from the other party or parties and will hold it on the same terms. When the mediation is completed, we will refund any portion (other than the administration fees, which are not refundable) not required to compensate the mediator and to pay DMI's expenses as discussed in these rules.

MEDIATION AND ARBITRATION OF DISPUTES ARISING UNDER THIS AGREEMENT

In the event a dispute arises between DMI or any mediator provided by DMI and any party, attorney, or other person involved in the mediation proceedings, which are related to the services of DMI, directly or indirectly, or the services of the mediator, directly or indirectly, such dispute will be handled first by mediation, and if mediation fails to succeed in producing an acceptable settlement of the dispute within ninety days from the date notice was given to DMI of the dispute, then by binding arbitration pursuant to the Florida Arbitration Code. Any conflicts between the Code and these Rules shall be resolved by following these Rules.

Mediation will proceed in accordance with DMI's Rules For Mediation. Arbitration will proceed in accordance with DMI's Rules For Arbitration, except that DMI will not select the arbitrator and no fees will be charged.

The arbitrators will be selected as follows: each party may choose an arbitrator, and must do so within ten days following the date mediation is terminated. These arbitrators will meet and will select a third arbitrator, who will be the chief arbitrator.

CONCLUSION

Thank you for using our services! We would appreciate your suggestions for further streamlining our processes.

APPENDIX B

Sample clauses for an agreement to mediate and arbitrate a future (possible) dispute

MEDIATION/ARBITRATION, ATTORNEY'S FEES:

In order to minimize the expense and difficulty of resolution of disputes related to this contract, informal mediation and binding arbitration are the only procedures which will be used to resolve disputes between the parties unless (Company) shall determine that it has an insurance contract containing a clause granting the insurer the right to control the settlement and litigation process, which contract covers the claim, in which case (Company)'s insurer will have sole discretion to determine whether this paragraph shall apply to such dispute. Should any dispute concerning any aspect of this contract arise between the parties, such disputes shall be settled first by conducting mediation, and then by referral to arbitration as hereafter provided. Either party shall give notice to the other and to Dispute Management, Inc., at its current mailing address as found on www.dispute-management.com, ("DMI") of the existence of a dispute and a desire to commence dispute resolution proceedings. Both parties will continue to discuss the dispute, even though a party has given notice to the other of intention to mediate and arbitrate. Mediation, then arbitration of any matters unresolved by mediation, will proceed in accordance with the provision of Chapter 44.301, Fla. Stats., et seq., and in accordance with Rule 1.700. et seq. and in accordance with DMI's Rules, all of which are made a part of this contract; and we agree to binding arbitration of future disputes as per the Florida arbitration statutes, even though there is no pending civil dispute at this time. In the event of any conflict between DMI's Rules and applicable Statutes and Rules of Civil Procedure, DMI's Rules will govern, unless to do so will invalidate the agreement to mediate and arbitrate, in which case local Statutes and Rules will apply. DMI will provide a mediator, and if required an arbitrator who is a lawyer admitted to practice in the courts in the State of Florida. Agreements reached by the parties through mediation shall be in writing, signed by the parties, and shall be binding upon the parties. Any award by an arbitrator will be in writing, signed by the arbitrator, and will be binding upon the parties. Each party will pay their own attorney's fees and costs independently incurred. The fees and costs charged by DMI for mediation and arbitration will be evenly divided between the parties. Both parties agree that a deposit equal to DMI's estimated hearing costs will be paid prior to the mediation hearing and any required arbitration hearing. If a party has paid more than their share of the mediation fees and costs, the other party shall reimburse them on demand. Should either party decide to contest any ruling of DMI, all costs, including attorneys' fees incurred by DMI and the other parties, will be the responsibility of the plaintiff. Orange County, Florida will be the exclusive venue and jurisdiction for resolution of all disputes, by whatever process. **The parties understand that they are giving up all rights to have a court, judge or jury decide disputes between them and are giving up rights to appeal any decision of the arbitrator, should arbitration be required. They understand also that any settlement agreement reached at mediation and any award of the arbitrator will be binding and legally enforceable. Each party understands the importance of obtaining legal advice about the costs and benefits of these agreements. Each party may** consult an attorney for such advice within the next ten days. Either party may revoke the contract within which this clause is found within ten days of the contract date.

Appendix C

DMI's Rules For Arbitration

✦

(Courtesy of Dispute Management, Inc., DeLand, Florida. www.dispute-management.com)

Revised October 1. 2003

INTRODUCTION

The Rules for DMI's Modern Arbitration Project have been crafted to keep the process as simple and speedy as possible, consistent with having a fair hearing. Unless all parties agree to a modification of these Rules or to the selection of one of the options listed below, each of the "Rules" is binding. If you select an option in writing or agree to an amendment of the Rules, again in writing, and all parties sign the agreement and forward it to DMI, DMI will abide by your decision if not in conflict with the company's policies and government laws and policies applicable to your case. DMI also reserves the right not to permit amendment to the Rules, should the amendment have any economic impact on DMI's operations, or on the operations of the Arbitrators.

COMMENCING THE PROCESS

Three situations are likely.

One, the parties have agreed in a written contract or other document to arbitrate any disputes arising in connection with a contract or some other transaction. In this case, if either of the parties notifies DMI in writing of the desire to arbitrate a dispute, stating simply the nature of the dispute and the names, addresses, and telephone numbers of the opposing parties, DMI will begin the process of setting a hearing time, choosing an Arbitrator or Arbitrators (some agreements or "contracts" call for panels of three Arbitrators), and giving appropriate written notice to all concerned.

(If the document you signed calls for mediation first, then arbitration, DMI will not automatically schedule arbitration. Once the mediator or one of the parties notifies DMI that an impasse has occurred and the parties are unable to reach an agreement within the time allowed by DMI's Rules For Mediation, DMI will begin the arbitration process as required under these Rules For Arbitration.)

Two, it's possible that an agreement has been reached, orally or in writing, since the contract was entered. Often, parties wishing to control the cost of disputes and better manage them to swift conclusion will agree to arbitrate a dispute rather than permit it to fall into the courts and litigation. DMI will respond to your written or oral request for arbitration exactly as if you had agreed to arbitration in your original contract.

Three, it's possible that you don't know whether the other party will agree to arbitration or not. If you call us or write us, telling us about the dispute and giving us the name, address, and telephone number of the other parties, we'll contact them to see if they will agree to a quicker, less expensive process of dispute resolution. If they do, we'll notify you, prepare a simple agreement setting the arbitration (unless you or any attorneys involved would prefer to do this), then we will proceed with the selection of an Arbitrator or Arbitrators, and we'll begin the process of setting the time for the hearing.

If all parties have previously agreed to the arbitration, or at such time as all parties do agree to arbitration if there was no preceding agreement in writing about arbitration, the party requesting arbitration will deposit the sum of $250.00 with DMI, which is a non-refundable fee for opening the file, and commencing the arbitration process. The Arbitrator will have the authority to award total or partial reimbursement of this sum at the conclusion of the arbitration. Unless there are postponements or cancellations, there will be no other charges from DMI, except for the actual time of the Arbitrators in rendering their services in these proceedings and direct costs DMI incurs on your behalf in handling your case in accord with DMI's Rates (available on request from DMI). DMI's charges for postponements and cancellations are explained in the section on that subject, found later in these Rules.

USING LAWYERS IN ARBITRATION

We encourage you to use the services of a lawyer during arbitration and in preparation for arbitration. However, our Arbitrators have ample experience with dispute resolution processes, and lawyers are not required to make the system work. We do not require that anyone have a lawyer, but if one of the parties employs a lawyer, the other party or parties should seriously consider doing so.

Lawyers have detailed and specialized knowledge about dispute resolution and can be extremely helpful in resolving disputes.

SELECTION OF THE ARBITRATOR

If you've entered into a contract which provides that arbitration will take place according to the Rules of Dispute Management, Inc., as presently published, DMI will select an Arbitrator qualified to preside over your arbitration hearing. The Arbitrator will be a lawyer in good standing. The Arbitrator will have experience in the subject field in which the dispute occurs. Some of our Arbitrators are former judges, and can be specifically requested. If either party requests a former judge, DMI will assign one unless the other party objects to any additional cost which might be charged by the former judge, in which case DMI will allocate the costs to each party as the parties agree or will appoint an attorney Arbitrator at a lower rate.

Objections to the appointment of an Arbitrator and requests for the appointment of a judicial Arbitrator must be filed with DMI within five days of receiving notice of the appointment of the Arbitrator. Each party is entitled to reject one Arbitrator without stating any reasons for the rejection. DMI will immediately appoint another Arbitrator, according to these Rules.

Arbitrators' fees vary with their experience. Additionally, some Arbitrators charge for their travel time and expenses, as well as for meals and lodging while away from home on arbitration business. DMI keeps track of the various charges made by Arbitrators working through DMI. At your request, we will provide these categories of charges to you in advance so you will be aware of what charges might be incurred with the use of any Arbitrator.

Once an Arbitrator has been selected, we will at your request provide you with any resumé information we have on the Arbitrator so you can know more about this person before meeting them during the proceedings.

PRE-ARBITRATION PROCEEDINGS

In court cases, extensive discovery and the filing of many motions often precede the actual trial. A great deal of time and expense is consumed in this work, which in litigation is not only advisable, but is often in fact a simple requirement of handling the case.

Because you agreed to arbitration to reduce cost and delay, DMI's arbitration will permit the taking of only two depositions by each party. A corporate party shall furnish a witness with firsthand knowledge of the transaction which brought about the dispute. Depositions may not exceed two hours in length, unless all parties agree to a longer time. The Arbitrator may, after notice and a hearing permit additional depositions and additional time for a previously scheduled deposition when required to permit a full and fair hearing for your case.

Each party is required to advise the other of, and make available for inspection and copying, any documentary or tangible evidence that will be relied upon at the hearing, not less than thirty days before the hearing, unless such documents have been delivered to the opposing party as the result of a request to produce documents (see below) made during the arbitration proceedings.

Each party may be required by the other to answer not more than twenty-five written questions. Any subparts to a question are regarded as additional questions. The questions must be answered in writing, under oath, and the answers must be delivered to the asking party within ten working days from their delivery to the answering party. The Arbitrator may, after notice and a hearing, permit additional questions if convinced that they are required in order to provide the interrogator with information required to permit a full and fair hearing.

Any party may request in writing that other parties admit the truth of any stated fact. If the request is not responded to within ten days from the date of receipt by the party to whom the request was directed, the fact will be treated as "true" by the Arbitrator. If the fact is denied, or if the recipient of the request states they do not know the answer, and that knowledge is reasonably within the files or other information of the party requested to admit, the Arbitrator may award the cost of later proving such fact to any party successfully proving it.

Each party may make two requests for the production of documents from the other party. Not more than twenty-five discrete documents or categories of documents may be requested. Additional documents reasonably believed to be relevant to the matters submitted for award may be requested and shall be produced, if permitted by the Arbitrator, after notice and a hearing.

a. Production of documents not objected to will be completed by delivery of the documents to the requesting party's offices on or before ten days after the request for good cause The Arbitrator may extend this time by not more than twenty additional days after notice and a hearing.

Any party may file motions with the Arbitrator for Protective Orders and to Compel Discovery, and the Arbitrator shall grant the same if any of the interests of fundamental fairness, cost control, personal privacy, relevancy or materiality require that the Order be entered. The prime standard applied is to assure that each party will have available to it the information needed to assure a fair and complete hearing.

All hearings about discovery issues will be by telephone conference call, arranged for a mutually acceptable date and time at the cost of the moving party. The Arbitrator may waive this requirement when necessary for proper case administration.

Parties may select the following *options* by their written mutual agreement:

1. There will be no depositions, requests for production of documents, requests for admissions, or written questions of any kind permitted before the arbitration, or stated portions of this option will be applied and other forms of discovery permitted as specified by the parties in writing, signed by all parties and delivered to DMI not less than forty-five days before the arbitration hearing.

2. The Florida Rules of Civil Procedure will apply if the parties agree to voluntarily comply with discovery requests without the need of court enforcement.

3. The parties can agree to special methods of discovery and a discovery schedule, if placed in writing, signed by the parties, and delivered to DMI not less than forty-five days before the arbitration hearing.

4. The Florida evidence code, or other agreed code, will apply in all proceedings.

If a party fails to respond to the requests of the other party for discovery after a motion to compel has been granted by the Arbitrator as specified in the foregoing, the requesting party will be entitled to apply in writing to DMI for a default. The application will be delivered to both DMI and the opposing party. After a telephone conference call hearing at a mutually acceptable time and date, or a date set by the Arbitrator if the parties are unable to agree, DMI will enter a default against a no-complying party, resulting in a full award favoring the applying party. If compliance occurs within five days of the date of receipt by the allegedly non-complying party of the application by the opposing party, no default will be entered. Entry of the award will terminate the case as a pending matter.

All notices, motions and other applications and responses to applications shall be mailed by certified mail, return receipt requested, or by registered mail.

ESTABLISHING THE DATE, TIME, AND PLACE FOR THE HEARING

DMI will work with all the parties to attempt to set hearing dates that are acceptable to the attorneys, the parties, and others who may be presenting testimony during the arbitration hearing.

If, after five business days of efforts to find a mutually acceptable date, no date is found to be acceptable to all parties, then DMI will set the date not less than sixty days or more than 120 days in advance, giving written notice to all the parties of the time, date, and place of the arbitration hearing. DMI will consider the parties' discovery plans in setting the date or the hearing.

The minimum time that will be set for an arbitration hearing is four hours. If the parties believe that additional time will be required, DMI should be contacted and advised of the perceived need. All parties will be consulted before additional time is set.

CONDUCT OF THE HEARING

The Arbitrator, or chief Arbitrator if more than one Arbitrator is required by the parties, will have final authority in conducting the hearing. DMI's Arbitrators are trained in assuring due process to disputants. Everyone will have an adequate opportunity to talk, in an orderly way. Unless agreed otherwise by the parties, each witness will be permitted to speak in a narrative fashion, without unnecessary direct or cross examination.

No rules of evidence are applied in DMI arbitration proceedings unless the parties have agreed otherwise. However, DMI's Arbitrators are trained in law and in evidence (unless you have agreed to a non-lawyer Arbitrator) and will be aware of what evidence would have greater and lesser value as proof. Evidence may be excluded by the Arbitrator if found to be of only minor value in deciding the case.

The hearings are informal, speedy, and relaxed. The absence of detailed technical rules assures all parties that "trapping" and "sandbagging" will not happen as a result of the procedural structure of these hearings.

CONCLUDING THE HEARING

In the sole judgment of the Arbitrator, the hearings will be continued, recessed, or concluded. The Arbitrators will assure courteous treatment of the litigants, but will not permit the proceedings to be unnecessarily prolonged for any reason, including lack of adequate preparation on the part of any disputant or evidence which could reasonably have been anticipated, but was not.

THE AWARD

Within ten working days after the hearing has been completed, the Arbitrator will provide a draft of the award to each party or to their attorneys, if represented by lawyers. Within five working days after receipt of the draft, a party may make formal or informal objections to the language of the draft or its inherent concepts.

These objections and criticisms are for the purpose of assuring that mathematical or logical errors have not been made by an Arbitrator, which the Arbitrator would prefer to change before making the award final.

If the Arbitrator chooses to change the award in any respect, this shall be done within ten working days from the date of receipt of the last objection or criticism. If no change in the award is made within the permitted time period, the award is final at the end of this period.

If the Arbitrator chooses to make no change to the draft award, the Arbitrator will sign it and mail it to each of the parties not less than twelve working days following conclusion of the hearing.

ENFORCING THE AWARD

In Florida there are two ways to go about creating a court enforceable arbitration award.

For arbitration conducted completely out of court, consult the Florida Arbitration Code, Chapter 682, Florida Statutes.

Arbitration can also occur during a pending lawsuit. A binding arbitration pursuant to the Florida Rules of Civil Procedure can be ordered by the court when all parties agree or a contract provides for it. Enforcement of awards made in such proceedings is provided for by the Florida Rules of Civil Procedure.

If for any reason review of the Arbitrator's award is desired, review possibilities exist under both the Florida Arbitration Code and the Florida Rules of Civil Procedure, to the extent they provide for binding arbitration. Please consult these Rules for guidance.

Awards do not always require court enforcement. Court enforcement is an additional expense for the parties, and the likelihood of setting aside an arbitration award by attacking it in court is relatively small. By all means, consult your attorneys if you feel that the Arbitrator or Arbitrators have made a mistaken or misguided award.

CANCELLATIONS AND POSTPONEMENTS OF HEARINGS

When arbitration dates and times are reserved, you are not buying an "option" on the Arbitrator's time and DMI's resources, which you may choose to exercise or not. You are actually buying the committed date and hours for the hearing, and DMI's and the Arbitrator's commitments to provide themselves, unconditionally, for the time and on the date reserved. DMI has committed its resources to your arbitration during the period of time you have requested.

When an arbitration hearing date and time is scheduled, the Arbitrator is 100% committed to being present, barring acts of nature, serious illness or death. The Arbitrator or Arbitrators are not permitted to accept other work for this time.

If you should cancel your arbitration more than thirty days before the hearing, with the agreement of all parties, there will be no charge for the reserved time.

If you cancel or postpone within thirty days of the committed hearing time and DMI is able to find other arbitration or mediation work for the Arbitrator for all or a part of the reserved time period, then to the extent other work is found, there will be no charge for the committed time. To the extent DMI is unable to replace the committed work with new work, you will be invoiced for the difference.

When a cancellation or postponement occurs and an additional hearing is requested, the party (if one party's emergency brings about a cancellation or postponement) or the parties (when all parties have agreed to a cancellation or postponement) will deposit with DMI the additional total sum of $150.00 to cover DMI's additional costs for further processing of the case.

THINGS WE CHARGE FOR

We reserve the right to make reasonable and customary business charges for long copy runs, long distance telephone calls made at your request, FAX transmissions and receipts made for your convenience, and for any costs we advance for you or your hearing (such as conference rooms, refreshments, requested projectors, screens or other equipment you especially ask for).

HOW DMI IS PAID

Unless otherwise arranged with DMI, when you request an arbitration you will need to send DMI funds equal to the Arbitrator's reasonable estimate of the hours required for arbitration times the hourly rate DMI charges for the arbitrator, divided by the number of parties involved ($75 an hour up to $125 an hour for each party in a two party case, depending on the Arbitrator you choose), plus the administration fee of $250.00. We will collect a similar sum from the other party (except they will be charged no administration fee). When the arbitration is completed, we will refund any portion of the hourly fees not required to compensate the Arbitrator and DMI's expenses as discussed in these rules. The administration fees are not refundable, but the Arbitrator may order a losing party to reimburse a prevailing party for all or a part of the administration fee.

WHAT HAPPENS IF SOMEONE DOES NOT PAY DMI'S INVOICES?

DMI's invoices are due upon receipt. Payment must be made as soon as they are received. We will not attempt to set an arbitration hearing until the party requesting has paid our invoice for the administration fee and their portion of the deposit for the Arbitrator's fee. If the person or company against whom the claim is made does not pay their portion of the deposit for the Arbitrator's fee, an award will be entered in favor of the other party for the administration fee, all or a portion of the deposit for the Arbitrator's fee, and all or a portion of the award they are claiming. An arbitration will be held, without further notice to the defaulting party, at which the Arbitrator will determine what the award should be, based upon the evidence and argument submitted by claimant at the hearing. Upon collection of the award, DMI shall have a lien for the sums awarded to it by the Arbitrator, and the first sums collected shall be the property of DMI.

MEDIATION AND ARBITRATION OF DISPUTES ARISING UNDER THIS AGREEMENT

In the event that a dispute arises between DMI, or any Arbitrator provided by DMI, and any party, attorney, or other person involved in the arbitration proceedings which are related to the services of DMI—directly or indirectly—or the services of the Arbitrator—directly or indirectly—such dispute will be handled first by mediation, and if mediation fails to succeed in producing an acceptable settlement of the dispute within ninety days from the date notice was given to DMI of the dispute, then by binding arbitration pursuant to the Florida Arbitration Code. Any conflicts between the Code and these Rules shall be resolved by following these Rules.

Any such mediation will proceed in accordance with DMI's Rules for mediation. The mediator will not be an employee, officer, director, agent of, or otherwise connected with DMI. Arbitration will proceed in accordance with these Rules, except that DMI will not select the Arbitrator and no fees will be charged.

The Arbitrators will be selected as follows: each party may choose an Arbitrator and must do so within ten days following the date mediation is terminated. These Arbitrators will meet and will select a third Arbitrator, who will be the chief Arbitrator.

OUR HEARINGS MAY BE MADE CONFIDENTIAL

A stenographic or otherwise recorded record of binding arbitration proceedings may be made at a party's expense. If a party chooses to make such a record, all aspects of the proceedings shall be conducted "on the record" unless all parties agree to a portion of the proceedings occurring "off the record." Such an agreement must be placed "on the record." Arbitrators are not permitted to conduct any part of the proceedings off the record unless such an agreement has been placed on the record.

Any record made of a binding arbitration may be kept confidential if the parties request it. However, a party seeking review may use such record in seeking review of the award, but agrees to move for an "in camera" non-record review by the court addressed. If, after an in camera review, no cause is found for modification or invalidation of the award, the record will be returned to the party to be kept confidential. If the review results in modification or invalidation of the award, those portions of the record pertinent to the decision may be made part of the public record in the court file concerning the review. (There are legal limitations that make it impossible to keep some information confidential. Please consult an attorney or contact the local bar association's legal aid service.)

Hearings and conferences which are conducted by DMI are closed to the public. They are private proceedings, to be attended only by the disputants and parties, their attorneys, and any other trusted experts and advisors. All parties and their attorneys, by virtue of using the DMI dispute resolution process involved, agree unconditionally that the neutral (whether Arbitrator or mediator) will not be subpoenaed or summoned for any purpose nor at any time required to testify concerning the proceedings which were conducted. The parties understand that there are legal limitations on the confidentiality which may be accorded certain subjects, such as abuse of children, the elderly and the disabled.

All parties agree that by using a DMI dispute resolution process, DMI is not a necessary or proper party in any proceedings—judicial or administrative—relating to the matters in controversy in the utilized dispute resolution process, nor shall DMI or any Arbitrator operating for DMI in these proceedings be liable to any one for any act or omission to act in connection with the conduct of arbitration pursuant to these Rules.

CONCLUSION

Thank you for using our services! We would appreciate your suggestions for further streamlining our processes.

0-595-30493-1